Frank Gervasi,

foreign-affairs analyst for *Collier's* and one of the few really top-flight men in his field, was born in Baltimore in 1908. His father was a mechanical engineer, whose work took him to various parts of the northeast in turn. Young Frank travelled with him; and thus it happened that his schooling was divided between Philadelphia, Atlantic City, Vineland, N. J., Newark, N. Y., and Philadelphia a second time. In his last year in high school he became a sports writer for the Philadelphia *Inquirer*, and continued this work during a year at Drexel Institute and another at the University of Pennsylvania. Then his formal education ceased, and his career in journalism took over.

For several years he was with the Philadelphia *Record*, as sports writer, religious editor, business editor, police reporter and rewrite man. In 1931 he joined the Associated Press, and spent three years in the New York newsroom feeding the South wire and covering some of the more important stories of the time.

To Whom

PALESTINE?

FRANK GERVASI

To Whom PALESTINE?

D. APPLETON-CENTURY COMPANY, INC.
New York   London

FOR

SEAN AND TOMMY

ACKNOWLEDGMENTS

The author herewith acknowledges the invaluable assistance of Sam Cherr, Richard Hippelheuser and Evelyn Young in the preparation of this manuscript.

CONTENTS

CONTENTS

PROLOGUE: *PURELY PERSONAL*

You ought to know something about why a book is written and as much as possible about the writer. Only then can you make the necessary allowances for the author's personal convictions and evaluate his work properly. So, if you'll pardon me for a moment, I'll step up and speak my piece and then I'll step out again and never return unless my publisher's editors let their fat pencils slip over the perpendicular pronoun. I'll keep out of the way of the facts as much as humanly possible. I don't expect I'll succeed completely. You see, I love Jews.

I love Catholics, too, and Moslems and Protestants and lots of members of the Greek Orthodox faith whom I've met in wandering about the world for the past twelve years, mostly in the Mediterranean whose lambent light I love, too. Atavism, probably. My ancestors came from the Mediterranean, from Sicily.

No, I'm not a Jew, nor am I an Arab, although sometimes as I watch Tommy or Sean perpetrate some outrage or other against the code of behavior of civilized people, I wonder if a Bedouin didn't slip into an ancestral tent in the distant past to inject into the family bloodstream a few trillion corpuscles of wild blood suddenly finding expression in the mores of my children. They certainly sound like Arabs—a people who

1

can't even say "I love you" quietly but must shriek it.

I was raised with Jewish kids in the less desirable regions of South Philly and later, following a small but perceptible improvement in the family fortunes, lived with other Jewish boys and girls in the bourgeois milieu of Rochester, New York. They taught me how to use my fists in street fights, to eat stuffed fish, to like unleavened bread, how to laugh and to appreciate good music.

My first girl was a Jewish girl and my first male friend was also a Jew. Between them they stimulated an interest in music, in art and literature, and without knowing it set my hands to journalism, an exacting but satisfying trade. So I have much to be thankful to Jews for.

I am equally grateful to some Catholics I've known and to many Protestants. A very dear friend of mine is a Moslem Egyptian. I am indebted to him because he introduced me to the Koran, a fine book although not as interesting as the Bible. I discovered other good friends in Egypt, all Moslems. Once, at Drexel Institute of Technology where for a while I tinkered with the idea that I might want to be an engineer, I had a Shinto friend. His name was Sam Hatai and he was a Japanese, a very fine fellow with a weakness for Scotch whisky. I am not by any means an expert on Shintoism but from what I saw of Sam, which was a lot, I have at least a reasonable doubt of the theory currently abroad that all Shintoists are evil and that all Japs are bad. Just a reasonable doubt.

I trust, by now, that you will have begun to see why I'm writing this book. I believe the idea actually came to me while riding a train from Bronxville to Grand Central, some weeks before moving down to Washington. I was seated next to a lady, a fine lady, a neighbor of ours in Bronxville. She was wondering whether she'd go to Cape Cod or not that season. The old place where she always went, she said, was beginning to crowd up with "the chosen people." She had no prejudices, she insisted, only it was better not to be crowded by "the chosen people," didn't I think? I don't remember what I said to her. I believe I merely looked at her and I recall that the rest of the ride into Manhattan was very dull indeed.

Maybe I'm writing this book because on coming home from six years or so of war reporting I grew sick of real estate ads labeled "restricted" and of hearing conversations begin "... some of my best friends. ..." You see, I'd seen Jews die alongside Catholics and Protestants and Orthodox Greeks, and their blood, I assure you, is uniformly red. I didn't see any Arabs die in freedom's cause.

No, this isn't exactly an "objective" book on Palestine and if you're looking for an "objective" book you might as well put this back on the shelf and save your $2.50. But wait, what's objectivity, anyhow? Webster says it means viewing events, phenomena and ideas externally and apart from self-consciousness. An objective reporter would be one, according to Webster, who would be detached and impersonal.

I suppose objectivity by such a definition could apply to scientific phenomena, to the process of judging the artistic values of belles-lettres, a piece of sculpture, a painting, a musical work. It could apply in law and business, a murder case or a stock deal. I can be objective about any or all of those things. I can be objective about the Bretton Woods proposals, inflation, the United Nations Charter and the case of Argentina. I can't be objective about human beings. I just naturally take the side of the underdogs, of the oppressed and the weak.

That's why I went to Palestine for the first time in the winter of 1939-40 a pro-Arab. I hadn't ever heard the Arabs' side of the story and I'd figured that the dice had been loaded against them. I've since found out a lot to support my feelings for them, which is why I am still fond of Arabs, especially the toiling fellaheen, the peasants. They're among the world's most thoroughly exploited people. But I've also seen what's been done to the Jews.

Certainly the Arabs have a case. But so do the Jews. The British overlords of Palestine have a case, too, and I don't intend to ignore it nor that of the Arabs. I mean, in fact, to set down the arguments for all three. None, you'll find, is altogether right, none altogether wrong. The weight of the evidence, however, making the proper deductions for my own convictions about the Jews' case, is overwhelmingly in their favor.

One arrives at conclusions, unless one is a dope or a dupe, after examining the evidence, after having been subjected to the impact of arguments and after looking personally and intimately into the fors and againsts. I have reached in my own mind certain conclusions. Inescapably they are in favor of the Jews.

The important thing is to believe in your own mind and heart that Justice is being done in the settlement of any dispute. You arrive at Justice by subtracting all the evil from the good. You subtract all the arguments against a decision from all the arguments for it and what you have left is Justice. That's what I've done about Palestine. Maybe that's true objectivity, after all.

Usually when someone has said to me, "You ought to be more objective about the Jews," the person has really meant to say, "I hate Jews and I don't see why you like them." Well, this book isn't for such people anyhow.

Nor do I hope to tilt very effectively with mass bigotry. I pray only that I may reach a few of the unconvinced and the skeptical by bringing to them as concisely as possible the results of some six years' study of the problem of Palestine.

I say "study." I don't mean to use the word in the sense that a scientist or an historian "studies." I am a newspaperman with all of the newspaperman's shortcomings as a member of the human race. So this isn't a definitive work on Palestine. At best it's a summary of the case for a Jewish Palestine and at worst it'll tell you where the place is, who lives in it and why all the fuss about it.

FRANK GERVASI

PART ONE

CHAPTER I: *THE PROBLEM*

Whether Palestine shall belong to the Arabs or the Jews or both, remain a British mandate or become the ward of the United Nations is high on the agenda of civilization's unfinished business. An answer is imperative. It is not too much to say that to ignore the problem of Palestine is to ignore the whole problem of the peace.

There are a number of possibilities: Palestine can be given to the Jews, or to the Arabs, or to both to fight out their destiny. It can remain a British mandate or be mandated in trust to the new United Nations Security Organization. These are the solutions put forward by Zionists, Arab nationalists, British imperialists and some fifty-seven varieties of "experts" on Palestinian and Middle Eastern affairs.

We have even heard certain eminent American diplomats advocate that the Jews should be siphoned out of the Holy Land and sent to unspecified destinations to work out their destinies as best they can. The Jews would be left a spiritual capital in Jerusalem, a sort of Holy See of Judea, shared with the Moslem and other religions which claim Jerusalem as their own.

We have also heard talk of partitioning Palestine into contiguous Arab and Jewish states.

Which of these "answers" is workable? Any solution of

the problem totally in favor of the Arabs would be not only a violation of all the explicit and implicit promises made over the past quarter of a century to the Jews, but would constitute of itself a gross injustice to a people who have contributed enormously to victory over our recent Nazi and Fascist enemy.

Although the Arabs have contributed little or nothing to that common victory, any solution wholly favoring the Jews would be unjust to the Moslems now resident in Palestine.

Nor can Palestine remain a British mandate. The League of Nations, which gave the British that responsibility, no longer exists. Of all the schemes advanced, that which proposes a trusteeship to be jointly held by the United Nations is the most reasonable; yet it too is *not* a definitive resolution of the problem but only a postponement of an ultimate solution. This decision must be made to the satisfaction of all parties if the final peace is to be conclusive.

Such a solution can only be found in the creation of a Palestine wherein the Jews may have liberty of immigration and colonization and, with the Arabs, equal rights under law to worship, work and live as a free people.

It has been said that the Arabs would object violently to such an answer to the Palestine question. In fact, British Colonial Office advocates of the status quo have advanced the possibility of an Arab Holy War to exterminate Jewry as the principal reason for not living up to the pledges of the Balfour Declaration, just as they traditionally pursued the policy of playing Germany off against Russia. It might be well to dispose at once of this colossal bugaboo. What fighting may or will occur in Palestine will be principally between British troops and Jews with, of course, the Arabs helping the British. A widespread Arab uprising is a myth.

Not one single Arab country or possible combinations of countries could effectively fight the forces which Palestine can raise, arm and put into the field. Palestine has had twenty-five years to raise a secret army of some 60,000 men. These are well trained. At least 40,000 of them have, in addition to their underground training, served in the armed forces of His Britannic Majesty. They know how to use weapons, are skilled in the arts of sabotage and self-defense and, most important, they have a cause.

The thought of Arab violence in Palestine has been so thoroughly implanted in the minds of even American diplomats and statesmen that last August 16th President Harry S. Truman was moved to make his support of the creation of a Jewish state in the Holy Land conditioned upon assurances that it could be achieved without bloodshed. Well, let us see just how much physical force could be marshaled by the Arabs.

Egypt, for instance, has an army of only 22,000 poorly armed, half-trained conscripts, lacking the weapons required for effective warfare. Iraq is so weak militarily that when the Raschid Ali government tried to stage an Axis putsch back in the critical summer of 1942, a couple of British battalions were enough to crush it. Saudi Arabia is, if possible, even less of a military threat.

Syria and Lebanon cannot be reckoned as military forces. The day has long passed when riflemen afoot or on horseback can be called soldiers. Against any Arab force, the Jews could hurl grenades, mortar fire, machine-gun fire and bullets from cocked automatic weapons.

Actual military activity by Arab countries neighboring Palestine would occur only if it were instigated and supported by outside powers and then only if they knew that their physical opposition would be welcomed by those outside powers.

Let us not, then, ignore this one basic fact—there will be violence over the creation of a Jewish Palestine or an independent Palestine only if the Great Powers concerned will it. There will be bloodshed certainly if Jewish aspirations to nationhood are frustrated, if hundreds of thousands of homeless and stateless Jews are barred from entering Palestine, and if the democratic powers fail once again to redeem their pledges of twenty-five years' standing.

Peace has come to Palestine as it has to most of the people of the world. The farmers are returning to the soil, the skilled workers to their trades, the lawyers and doctors and business men to their offices. Their problem has been solved. This was to defeat Nazism and Fascism in its various European and Oriental expressions.

In varying degrees the problem was solved for foe as well as friend. Germans, Italians and Japanese, too, have been released from the miasmas of fear and insecurity generated by the regimes of their former rulers. While they may know cold and hunger for some time to come, they have nonetheless no irreconcilable compulsion to resort to physical violence unless frustration of their democratic impulses continues and becomes unbearably acute.

In any event most of the peoples involved in this war, victors and vanquished alike, have friends. Even the Fascists have friends and the Nazis do not find it difficult to arouse the sympathies of some elements among the Allied victors. Not so the Jews. Anti-Semitism is deeply rooted in the bigotry and prejudices of people. The defeat of Hitler and of Mussolini did not wipe out anti-Semitism. On the contrary, this ignoble emotion has enjoyed a postwar prosperity throughout Europe—and if the Bilbos of our own country are to be taken seriously, it finds something of a refuge in the hearts of some elements in our own society.

The unwanted Jews of Europe seem less able to find friends in England and America than ever before. Some two decades of Nazi and Fascist propaganda have done their work even in those strata of society where one would expect reason and tolerance to prevail.

For the European Jews who have no birth certificates, no passports, no homes and certainly no farms, trades or offices to which to return—for these, there is only Palestine. Does America offer a haven and a home? Does Britain?

No, there is no peace in Palestine nor can there be peace until the problem is solved. You might appropriately ask *why*. Why all this fuss about the Jew? Above all because the Jew is flesh and bone and blood, because he is a fellow-human, because he was the first victim of the Nazis and Fascists over whom we have won a physical victory, because the Jew has contributed his blood and wealth to that common cause. Later we shall assess the extent of the Jew's direct contribution to victory, although such a documentation should be superfluous for those who have seen the photographs and newsreel shots of the Nazi extermination camps at Belsen and Buchenwald.

It is, furthermore, essential to solve the problem of Palestine in the interests of a lasting peace. Geography assigned to Palestine a fateful role in the destiny of the Middle East, situated as it is on the flank of the British route through the Mediterranean to distant sources of raw materials and faraway markets for British goods. Palestine is a strategic territorial outpost of the British sphere of influence in the Levant, adjacent to the area of Russian interests in the Mediterranean, substantially less than three hours by bomber from the Dardanelles. It is one of the fulcrums of power politics in the eastern crescent of the Mediterranean. And because Palestine lies along the life-line of the British Empire it is more importantly a fulcrum of power politics of the world. Palestine need never be an area of contention between the World Powers. But diplomacy, like politics and business, had always been many years behind scientific progress.

The advent of the atomic bomb should have proved the obsolescence of nineteenth century concepts of strategy and diplomacy. Of what strategic use is Palestine to imperial Britain in an era of rockets, jet-propulsion and exploding atomic energy?

Frontiers were meaningful only when men marched afoot or moved in horse-drawn or motor-powered vehicles, when the distances between attackers and the attacked were sufficiently great. Today space and time have been reduced to minimums. An attack may be set into motion and reach its objective through the simple process of pressing a button.

Frontiers, territorial bulwarks, groupings of states and nations as buffers between potential belligerents are as obsolete as the diplomacy of *cordons-sanitaires*. High-speed airplanes had already outmoded them, although generals and diplomats did not admit it. They must admit now the obsolescence of their techniques and their concepts of battle and diplomacy. "Palestine," the British say, "is essential to the defense of the Suez Canal." To this a scientist would answer: "Rubbish."

Imperialists also argue that they cannot yield the oil sources near Palestine. True, but only so long as the scientific processes which produced an atomic bomb fail to produce atomic engines. It is foreseeable that well within a quarter of a century atomic energy may displace the oil which now seems so indispensable to modern life. But, of course, it is too much to expect civil servants and career diplomats and business men to see too far into the future. Their record to date is a monument to shortsightedness, not one to vision.

We must deal with the problem of Palestine as it is and not as it might be a quarter of a century hence, just as we must, in considering the whole world, arrive at the decisions of peace based upon conditions now—not of tomorrow. And the problem as it is stems out of the quarrel between the Jews, to whom it *was* promised as a homeland, and the Arabs, who lay claim to it by virtue of prior possession, complicated by the desire of the British to hold on to it as long as possible.

It was hoped, when a Labor government came to power in England, that a more friendly atmosphere would be created for the growth of the aspirations of the Jews to nationhood. It soon became obvious that such hope was unfounded. Mr. Ernest Bevin, the British Foreign Minister, obviously is no more willing to live up to the pro-Zionist pledges of Great Britain than his Tory compatriot, Mr. Winston Churchill.

If anything, in spite of past declarations of sympathy for the Jewish case by the Labor party and the trade unions, the present British government is more obdurate than ever. For this there are good and abundant reasons—not the least of which is the poverty of the United Kingdom following the long and costly recurrence of the Great War of the Twentieth Century. No government in Britain today, Labor or otherwise, can afford to go to its people with any proposition indicating a yielding anywhere of possible trade outlets if such a relinquishment might further burden the already overtaxed British people.

In this the United States, long a lip-servant to Zionism and to movements for a Jewish Palestine, has been of little help. Congress and the American people have shown a vast reluctance to help their wartime Allies financially, although such help is essential to the regeneration of trade and to the construction of a lasting peace. A loan by a New York bank to a British manufacturer and the problem of Palestine are more intimately related than one would believe. A Britain with a reasonable hope of restoring its position in world trade and so providing a minimum of security for its miners and industrial workers, would be a Britain more disposed to freeing Palestine and to liberalizing its imperial policy generally.

Either we are to have a world in which trade shall flow freely and the masses of workers everywhere shall attain those minimum economic guarantees essential to well-being and peace, or we shall continue to limp along, erecting trade barriers, devaluing currencies, competing in world markets, creating monopolies and otherwise proceeding toward another recurrence of war.

Since considerations of profit and self-interest seem still to be paramount in international relations, it is the intention of this small book to show that nationhood for Palestine will bring benefits in the only coin our governments seem to understand—profitable trade. They may wish to overlook completely the moral aspects of the Palestinian question. They cannot ignore the practical ones.

A Palestine wherein the Jews may have free scope for their agricultural and industrial aptitudes means a Palestine in which Jews and Arabs can earn more money, create wealth and so increase the buying power of the people and with it the amount of goods which the industrial giants may sell there.

In their seventy years of work in Palestine, the Jews have shown that they can make the desert bloom and can build great industries, great cities and good schools, universities, hospitals and roads. They have raised the economic level of Palestine so that both Jew and Arab have prospered.

The immigration of Arabs into Palestine has increased considerably since the first Jewish settlers arrived. Their wages have gone up. They prefer to live in Palestine rather than in Egypt or Iraq, Iran or Saudi Arabia. The reason is simple: in Palestine, thanks to the influence of educated, progressive Jews, Arabs are better off than they are anywhere else in the Moslem world. Naturally, their leaders will not admit this. Pashas, not peasants, own the oil wells of the Middle East and receive from their British and American patrons the royalties and other emoluments of the oil racket.

Until a worldwide oil cooperative is formed—until, in short, oil is internationalized—the sticky black stuff that comes up out of the desert will remain a source of international discord. Palestine itself has little or no oil but is important in the petroleum picture as the terminus of the pipe-lines which carry oil to shipping points at Haifa and other Holy Land ports.

The oil companies are interested in having a friendly Palestine and the British government should be. This should be, in fact, an underlying consideration of all concerned in dealing with the question. A friendly Palestine could be achieved by giving it independence. As it is now Palestine is an unfriendly, disillusioned land where Jews are determined to fight for fulfilment of the promises of the Balfour Declaration.

There is reason to believe, however, that the powers are less interested in peace and security in Palestine than they are in dividing and ruling, in pitting Arab against Jew and ultimately avoiding a solution which would give Palestine sovereignty. This is a shortsighted and criminal policy. The avoidance hitherto of any solution which would satisfy in whole or in part Jewish claims to the Holy Land can mean only that in the large sense, Adolf Hitler has won the war. It means that the Jew shall remain forever in the ghetto.

One of the great lies perpetuated by those who want no peace in Palestine is that the Jew and the Arab cannot live side by side in peace. Left to their own devices, plain Arabs find little fault with plain Jews. The two quarrel only when inspired by extremists of one or the other side or when instigated by those who "own" the Arab leaders lock, stock and caftan.

The elements of the quarrel are such that if we continue to blunder along, bloodshed in Palestine is inevitable. It would not be surprising if by the time this book reaches print Palestine should be in the throes of a civil war, as fierce as any that we have known in the past quarter of a century. The moral issues involved are as profound as those of the struggle of the Irish nation to emerge as a sovereign people. The actual physical character of the struggle, too, will be similar. Jews will be pitted against British troops just as Irish patriots were pitted against the Black and Tans back in the days of The Trouble.

The Palestine question, in fact, more nearly resembles the Irish one psychologically than any other in modern history. In dealing with Palestine as with Ireland, the British have seemed to be congenitally unable to comprehend the spiritual issues involved. Whenever they are confronted with a physical problem our Anglo-Saxon friends seem eminently able to cope with it, though it might be as staggering a one as that of crushing Nazi-Fascism despite overwhelming odds. Hitler and Mussolini, as before them Napoleon, were somehow beaten. But when faced by Irishmen possessed with the notion that they shall be free, or by Jews as fervently aspiring to sovereignty, the British have been helpless.

This is probably because in their own hearts the British know the virtues of the case for freedom. They themselves love it so well. They cannot fight whole-heartedly to prevent others from achieving it. They might try to delay the end, employing force if necessary. They will indubitably employ it in Palestine as they did in Ireland, but their hearts won't be in it. For after all it is always the people who fight, and there are no more decent freedom-loving people in the world than those who sacrificed enormous quantities of life and treasure in what seemed at the outset a hopeless struggle against the Nazis and the Fascists.

That strife will come inexorably because the forces at work are greater than armies. Ever since Palestine was given to the British in mandate by the League of Nations, Jews have sought to achieve the promises of the Balfour Declaration through peaceful negotiations, reason and logic. They have also employed the weapons of propaganda. The Zionists, for whom the religious considerations of millenia of history in the Holy Land are powerful and moving, have been particularly cir- cumspect in striving toward the establishment of a National Home. But the Jewish terrorists have been less than circumspect and have used the weapons of violence rather than those of persuasion.

So long as it seemed possible that logic and reason could prevail, Palestine—except for minor incidents and clashes—was comparatively peaceful, but as with the increasing adamancy of the British leaseholders it became clear that *evolutionary* strategy and tactics were futile, the *revolutionary* movement has grown.

There have since been strikes and bloodshed and increasing evidence that the Jewish temper is growing short. More and more the moderate Jews have lost followers to the extremist group. Every one of the Jews who fought in North Africa and Italy and elsewhere in Europe as a member of the British armed forces and who has returned to Palestine is now a potential revolutionary, not because he wants to be, but because he has seen the Promised Land denied to the Jews as a refuge by the British White Paper of 1939, because he has no longer much hope that his people's dream can be realized by temperate means. He is ready now to fight and to die in his cause.

Such a struggle could easily wreck the new machinery created at San Francisco for the maintenance of peace, just as the Manchurian Incident and the Fascist war upon Ethiopia ruined the fragile peace enforcement devices of the League of Nations.

A conflict in Palestine could reasonably bring about a clash between the Soviets and the Western powers, for the Middle East is a center of worldwide air communications, a crossroads of Great Power interests.

Obviously the Palestine problem must be solved. The solution demands the immediate opening of Palestine to unlimited Jewish immigration until the absorptive capacity of the country has been exhausted. Once that has occurred—preferably under the trusteeship of the United Nations until the necessary economic, social and political readjustments have been made—Palestine should be allowed to grow and expand at the will of those natural economic and political forces thus set into motion.

In the end there is no doubt that the Jews will prevail and that they will predominate in industry and agriculture and politics. They are intellectually better equipped than the Arabs for these pursuits. But there is no reason to believe that a people who themselves have known bondage, persecution and worse will impose upon Arab co-nationals any system of government wherein they would not be permitted the fullest possible individual rights.

The destiny of the Arabs would be safe in a sovereign Palestine, even in a Jewish Palestine. The rights of the Jews in an Arab Palestine might on the other hand be seriously endangered, for nowhere in the Middle East, nowhere in the entire Moslem world—which reaches from Morocco on the Atlantic across Africa and Araby, India and Southeastern Asia, into the lower Philippines —have the Arabs demonstrated aptitude for any kind of government recognizing the freedom of the individual. Only in those regions where the Arab has been permitted a minimum of economic security, education and sanitation is there any semblance of Arab individualism and of Arab aspiration to democracy.

In an independent Palestine, instead, the Arab, afforded equal rights to work and the benefits of education and sanitation, can ultimately emerge (if he can overcome the essentially reactionary dogma of his religion) as a free man.

To understand the problem of Palestine, its relation to the problems of the Middle East and to those of the Mediterranean, we must know the land and its people, recognize the economic and political forces at work and above all the moral issues concerned.

If at times this book descends to the level of a primer in describing the country and its inhabitants and the nature of the forces at large among them, it is in the interests of understanding a complex subject that has become obfuscated by emotions and partisanship.

I have tried, perhaps not always successfully, to avoid both. I write only on the basis of what I have learned through first-hand experience.

Let us look at the existent situation created by the struggle between the Jewish antagonists over whether evolutionary or revolutionary methods should be pursued in the effort to create a Palestinian nation. Once aware of the nature of this struggle and its threat to the peace, we can go back to how and why it all started.

CHAPTER II: *TERROR*

Walter Edward Guinness, first Baron Moyne of Bury St. Edmunds, was a slim, pallid man who looked like a retired character actor—urbane, handsome and restrained. Had Lord Moyne devoted himself to making the stout for which his Dublin family became famous, instead of entering politics and diplomacy, he would almost certainly be alive today. For he would not have been in listless, fragrant Cairo in November, 1944.

But Lord Moyne wasn't an actor and he didn't pay much attention to the brewery industry. He was the British Resident Minister in the Middle East, the instrument of British imperial policy in those trouble-charged lands.

Lord Moyne was, therefore, a man marked for death. His assassination was a predictably probable act of Palestine terrorism, not because he was Moyne, but because he was the symbol of British policy in the Middle East.

On the afternoon of November 6, 1944, while Cairo lay in its customary midday torpor, Lord Moyne was shot and killed by two assassins hiding in the shrubbery of his modern Mediterranean villa. The shots mortally wounded Moyne, killed his soldier-chauffeur outright and almost literally echoed around the world. They were intended to. They were fired by Jewish terrorists.

24

The killers were Eliahu Hakim and Eliahu Bet-Tsouri, twenty and twenty-three years old respectively, members of the so-called Stern Gang, the smaller but more virulent of two terrorist organizations operating in Palestine. They were captured by an Arab policeman. Egyptians tried, prosecuted, defended, judged and subsequently sentenced the pair of young killers to death by hanging. They received, according to the law, what they deserved.

Their fate didn't, however, solve the problem of terrorism in Palestine. Much less did it solve the greater problem of Palestine itself.

Hakim's and Bet-Tsouri's confessed motive for the murder of Moyne was to arouse world opinion about Palestine. From the witness stand in the noisy, hot, Cairo courtroom, Hakim and Bet-Tsouri, carefully briefed by their terrorist leaders in what to say and even how to say it, told why they killed Moyne. The correspondents covering the trial for the world press were not permitted to report what Hakim and Bet-Tsouri said. They were not even allowed to make notes.

The killers sought to put Great Britain's imperial and colonial policy in Palestine on trial at a critical moment in world history. Because of censorship, the young terrorists failed in their propagandist mission and so wasted the lives of Moyne, his driver and themselves. In the end they were tried—and not Britain.

In one sense, however, Hakim and Bet-Tsouri succeeded. They indirectly but effectively brought Palestine to public notice once again. The problem of Palestine or, as it's sometimes called, "the Jewish question," had been shoved into the background by the war.

But statements by British and Jewish officials condemn-
ing terrorism and deploring politics by murder could
not alter the issues contained in the conflict any more
than they could restore Moyne to life. These issues have
challenged the political ingenuity and patience of British and Jewish officials ever since the Balfour Declaration—admittedly as ambiguous a document as ever was
written—promised the Jews a national home in Palestine.

The trouble began on November 2, 1917, when
Arthur James Balfour wrote Lord Rothschild:

His Majesty's Government view with favour the establishment in Palestine of a national home for the Jewish
people, and will use their best endeavors to facilitate the
achievement of this object, it being clearly understood that
nothing shall be done which may prejudice the civil and
religious rights of existing non-Jewish communities in Palestine, or the rights and political status enjoyed by Jews in
any other country.

This statement was issued in the name of the British
War Cabinet. It was confirmed by a joint resolution of
the Sixty-seventh Congress of the United States, approved by President Woodrow Wilson and incorporated
in the League mandate. The World Zionist Organization, charged with the development of Jewish interests
in the Holy Land, went to work. Jews were brought in
from the ghettos of Central, Eastern and Southeastern
Europe. They built cities like Tel Aviv, towns like
Ramat Hakovesh. They made deserts blossom into
farms, banana plantations and citrus orchards. They
built factories, and Palestine—Arab and Jewish—prospered.

The population of Palestine in 1922 totaled 589,177 Arabs and 83,790 Jews. By the spring of 1939, the Arab population had doubled to about one million, while the Jews had increased sixfold to about 550,000.

London felt it had to appease the Arabs who opposed the influx of Jews to Palestine. In May, 1939, the government of the champ appeaser of our time, Mr. Neville Chamberlain, issued the White Paper closing Palestine to Jewish immigration. At the moment, some six million European Jews stood in the path of Hitler's armies. Ever since, Palestine's Jews and their Zionist supporters everywhere have been fighting to have the White Paper revoked and the country reopened to immigration.

Whether or not the Balfour Declaration legally permits unlimited Jewish immigration is another matter. Any good Zionist lawyer can find words in Balfour's historic paragraph to mean yes, and his Arab counterpart can find some to mean no. The legal technicalities seem to me far less important than the human aspects of the problem. There is, certainly, sufficient legal basis in the declaration to open the gates of the Promised Land to the Jews. Standing outside those gates are some 2,000,000 homeless, cold, hungry, sick and stateless Jews. They wander over Europe among the ruins and many still call "home" only the concentration camps where the Nazis put them.

Their plight has aroused the peaceable people of Palestine, and the conflict over their fate is nearing a climactic explosion far more dangerous to peace in the Middle East and to United Nations unity than the one which flared in Syria and Lebanon last summer. Denied representation at the San Francisco Conference,

Jewish hopes of achieving independence through political and diplomatic means have nearly expired. While
the Jews were not permitted to have representatives at
San Francisco, the Arabs were. One of their delegates
was Faid Zain Ed Din, a former Axis agent in Syria
and collaborator and friend of the infamous Baldur
Von Schirach, the German Youth leader. Faid set up
the Arab Club in Damascus and was a projection of
Nazi influence in Islam. He was so notoriously an enemy
of democracy that he was interned by the British when
they were obliged to liberate Lebanon and Syria from
Vichy by force. He was released when Syrian independence was proclaimed. His presence at San Francisco did
little to encourage the hopes of moderate Jews for a
peaceful settlement of the Palestine conflict.

David Ben Gurion, chief of the executive body of
the Jewish Agency, has warned that Jewish patience is
at an end and that the Jews will resort to "direct means"
at any moment. If last-minute efforts to obtain a pacific
solution in Palestine fail, then a general strike, violence,
revolution and civil war can be expected.

Of the world's 17,000,000 Jews, some 5,000,000 have
been slaughtered in Europe by the Nazis. The Jews
count their dead, measure their war effort in the soldiers
they have given to the common cause, the money and
work they have contributed—and feel that they have an
unquestionable claim to nationhood.

Both the Stern Gang and its bigger brother, the Irgun
Zevai Leumi, or National Military Organization, seek
to foment civil war and eventually revolt against Britain.
That is the terrorist "solution" for the Palestine problem.
Ultimately the objective of the Zionists and of the ter-

rorists is the same: Jewish nationhood. But whereas the Zionists hope to accomplish it through legal, democratic, political and diplomatic means, the terrorists demand a short cut. They want to throw the British out by force and to establish a Jewish Free State. They're the Sinn Feiners of Judaism in revolt. Friedman-Yellin, the present leader of the Stern Gang, is a square-faced, blue-eyed fanatic who has transplanted to Palestine the gangster technique of the Capones and the O'Bannions of our terrible twenties.

Yet neither Friedman-Yellin nor Menachem Begin, the skinny, pasty-faced former law student who heads the other terrorist organization, the N. M. O., can be written off as a pair of bloodthirsty thugs. Maybe they are personally, and so are a good many of their followers. For the most part, however, the terrorists are misguided, fanatic patriots, and their methods must be seen against the background of Palestine, where some half-million Jews were forced to sit on their hands while their relatives in Europe were slaughtered.

The Stern Gang was organized some years ago—nobody seems to know just when—by a Polish Jew named Abraham Ben Mordecai Stern. The gang grew out of a secret society which called itself the Fighters for Freedom of Israel, a small group of desperadoes and jailbirds specializing in individual terrorism. The gang was responsible for the attempt on the life of former High Commissioner Sir Harold MacMichael last summer, and for killing Assistant Superintendent of Police Wilkin. The gang's business is murder. Its leader learned the trade in tough schools—prewar Poland and Fascist Italy.

A Zionist who knew Stern described him to me as

an able, single-minded and singularly stubborn man. He arrived in Palestine from Russia as a boy of fifteen, attended secondary schools and the university in Jerusalem, and then went to Poland and later to Italy where he became an admirer of Benito Mussolini.

"The British are our enemy as much as the Germans," he often said. "The Germans kill Jews, and the British don't do anything to save them." He lived by this credo, made it the battle-cry of his small, mobile band.

On the softer side, Stern wrote creditable poetry and was married to a professional pianist, who bore him one child, didn't agree with him politically but loved him devotedly. He allowed himself a salary of only six pounds sterling (about twenty-four dollars) a month.

The Stern Gang is organized with emphasis on secrecy. No member is supposed to know more than a handful of the others. Less than 10 per cent of the members are Palestinian-born, many of them being Polish Jews. The links between Palestine terrorist activity and prewar anti-Semitism in Poland are many and curious. Stern had organized a revolutionary secret society in Poland. When war came, these men entered the Polish army. Captured by the Russians on the Eastern front, they were released and made their way to Palestine. There the former Stern Gang members deserted the Polish army and rejoined the terrorists.

Stern was killed in 1942, when he was about thirty-five years old, while he was hiding in a house in Tel Aviv. To the terrorists he is a martyr who must be avenged. Stern left to Friedman-Yellin a gang numbering some forty to fifty so-called "front men" or trigger men, and one hundred and fifty "helpers"—informers, stooges and assistants of one kind and another, including expert pamphleteers.

The more serious and the stronger of the two terrorist groups is in the National Military Organization. The N. M. O. recently split with the Revisionist party, in order to train youths in the art of guerrilla warfare, sabotage and terrorism. How many have been graduated from the N. M. O.'s school few know, but persons in Cairo able to estimate the organization's strength with some accuracy told me that it can count at the moment on some three hundred to four hundred trigger men and at least two thousand "helpers."

While the Sternists single out key men for their victims, the N. M. O.'s technique is to strike directly at the British administrative machinery in Palestine. One organization supplements the work of the other, but whereas the Stern hoodlums seem to be satisfied with martyrdom, the N. M. O. boys are far more ambitious. They don't want to die fighting. They want to live victoriously. They want to rule Palestine.

Less extreme than the Sternists, the members of N. M. O. tried to avoid committing any act of terrorism which would impede the war effort. In their pamphlets and propaganda, for instance, they urged Jews to join the British army. Volunteers from their ranks gave valuable help to the British in the suppression of the pro-Axis revolt in Iraq in 1941.

The pattern of N. M. O. terrorism is to blow up the offices of the Palestine government's Immigration Department as a protest against the restriction of Jewish immigration under the White Paper; to plant bombs in the headquarters of the Palestine police, enforcers of the White Paper policy, but not to touch the British military police. Whenever actual British troops or British police might become involved in a terrorist project, the N. M. O. "helpers" tip them off by telephone.

A source of power for the N. M. O. is the Poles—that section of the Polish army known as the Dwoika, or secret service. The links between the N. M. O. and the Poles are more numerous, more easily identifiable than those between the Sternists and the Poles. There existed until just before the war a sort of unholy alliance between Polish anti-Semitic elements and extreme Jewish nationalists directly or indirectly linked to the N. M. O. Polish pressure against Jews created candidates for admission to Palestine, a state of affairs which enabled the extremists to bring pressure to bear on the British, in turn, for permission to allow the persecuted Polish Jews to enter the Promised Land.

This entente was rudely violated by the Poles when they instituted actual pogroms against the Jews. Not even Palestine's extremists could take this, although the mass murders served their propaganda purposes and intensified the clamor to allow free immigration of Jews to Palestine. Like Stern, the leader of the N. M. O., Menachem Begin, was "formed" in Poland. A squinty, unprepossessing fellow, he was born there, studied law at Warsaw University and served in the Polish army.

When Polish troops were evacuated from Russia to the Middle East by way of Palestine in 1941-42, connections among the Palestinian Revisionist Party, the

N. M. O. and their Polish confrères of the old days were re-established. They had new reasons, now, to resume business.

The right-wing Poles fear and hate Russia and communism. Their Dwoika, or secret service, enlisted the help of the N. M. O. and the Revisionists in identifying pro-Russian elements in the Polish army. They also asked the Revisionists to help them disseminate anti-Russian and anti-communist propaganda through their well-established channels in Britain and the United States. In return, the Poles promised and gave invaluable help to the N. M. O. terrorists.

According to one important source the Poles furnished the N. M. O.: (1) instructors to teach terrorists how to use firearms and explosives; (2) transportation of weapons and explosives in Polish military staff cars; (3) refuge in their military camps for N. M. O. members sought by the police. It was a simple matter for the Poles to detach officers "for special duty," and an undeterminable number were released to the N. M. O. to drill and lead the terrorists. British Palestine police, searching for weapons and dynamite, couldn't question the presence of such equipment in regular Polish army vehicles, and they didn't even think of looking for escaped terrorists in British battle dress in Polish army camps.

The British eventually realized what was going on. The Poles made it plain that they were cross with the British, feeling that they were being "betrayed" on the altar of Allied unity with Russia. When the British dug into the causes of Polish rancor, they uncovered, among other things, the links between the Poles and the N. M. O., but by this time the harm had been done.

Between the arrival in Palestine of the first refugee Poles in 1941-42 and June of 1944, the rhythm of N. M. O. and Sternist terrorism increased. On May 18, 1944, three truckloads of armed terrorists invaded the Palestine Broadcasting System's station at Ramallah, near Jerusalem. Police cars found the roads leading to the station blocked by land mines. On another morning a Jewish policeman was found dead on his doorstep. Nearly every morning Palestinians found walls covered with posters calling for riot and rebellion. Extortions to finance the N. M. O. were traced to the terrorists. The police arrested hundreds of suspects. Zionist organizations and the Jewish Agency instituted an independent land-wide manhunt, but terrorism continued, practically unchecked.

By the end of October, less than a month before Hakim and Bet-Tsouri fired their fatal slugs at Moyne, terrorism and repressive measures had reached a fearful climax. Raids on settlements where terrorists might be harbored were an everyday occurrence. On October 26th, for instance, the village of Nathanya was raided by police and military authorities, six hundred and fifty Jewish settlers were interrogated, fifty were detained. Another nine hundred were questioned the next day and twenty-two arrested. About three hundred arrested suspects were shipped to concentration camps in distant Eritrea and Khartoum.

The deportations aroused the New Zionist party's anger. The New Zionists (not to be confused with the Zionists) are an offshoot of the old Revisionist party founded in 1929 by the late Messianic, Russian-born Vladimir Jabotinsky. They consistently advocated a much sterner policy towards Britain and were uncompromising in their demands. In recent years they warned that civil war threatened Palestine if the Jewish Agency cooperated with the British in wiping out terrorism. They called on the Palestine government to revoke deportation of actual or suspected terrorists and aroused Jews to a countrywide protest against their arrest.

In view of the situation, it was surprising that Lord Moyne was not better guarded than he was. In Cairo, in those days, I talked with the Jewish Agency executives about what might happen in Palestine. They were worried and depressed. One of them said sadly, "The present state of affairs cannot endure. Organized elements of the Zionist movement have reached the point where they will need to act against the terrorists—and soon."

To "act against the terrorists" means that decent Jews must turn informers against their own people. Informers in any such situation are doomed men and no matter how much they may deplore the violence of the terrorists, the Jews feel that the Sternists and the members of the N. M. O. are fighting, ultimately, their fight. They are reluctant to turn them in.

The Jews obtain little help from the highly touted Palestine police, composed largely of British but with some Arab and Jewish members. In spite of handsome publicity to the contrary, they are about as inefficient a police organization as it's possible to find anywhere. The Zionists blame much of the terrorism on their laxity. They allowed some twenty known terrorists, for example, to escape from the well-guarded Latrun prison and others to break out of the Acre prison. They never seem to be able to keep terrorists behind bars, and law-abiding Jews in Palestine ask themselves whether the Palestine police really want to stamp out terrorism.

Following Moyne's murder, the drive to crush terror-ism in Palestine intensified. The Jewish Agency's lead-ers—Moshe Shertok, David Ben-Gurion and others on up to Dr. Chaim Weizmann, head of the Zionist move-ment—declared open warfare on the terrorists, many of whom, notwithstanding their laws of secrecy and their juvenile blood-brotherhood stuff, are known to every-day citizens. Even if the inner antagonisms within Pales-tine don't reach the terrorist "ideal" of mass rebellion against the British, there is certain to be bloodshed. Some two thousand to three thousand well-armed des-perate men can easily precipitate civil war.

The possibility of an armed uprising of Jews to ob-tain a National Home in Palestine is no longer remote. It will happen if and when all other means, political and diplomatic, fail.

It is foreseeable that the activist view of the terrorists rather than the passive attitude of the Zionists may pre-vail. The appointment of Lord Gort (who has since resigned for reasons of health) as High Commissioner in place of Sir Harold MacMichael, indicated the British were aware of the dangers to peace that Palestine pre-sents. Their experience in Greece was a bad one; a similar occurrence in Palestine would be much worse.

Such are the dimensions of the physical conflict brew-ing in Palestine. Can the peace structure withstand the impact of such a conflict? Can it not be avoided and the problems settled in justice to all concerned? I believe they can and they must be so settled. For those who are swayed only by legal facts, there is an abundance of juridic evidence for the creation of an independent state in Palestine. The moral evidence too is quite ample.

CHAPTER III: *HEROES*

The ill-temper of moderate as well as extremist Jews arises out of a growing sense of outraged justice. Put yourself into the shoes of a Palestinian Jew. You were called up when war came. You wanted to fight, if possible, in a Jewish army under your own flag, but you were denied this privilege. You were offered service in the regular army of His Majesty's Government. You were called and you went.

For four, five or six years you fought outside Palestine, saw service in Egypt, Libya, Sicily, Italy and France. You served as a truck driver, a member of an engineer battalion or a supply regiment in Africa or India. You did the most menial jobs and you seldom, if ever, met the hated enemy face to face. Once when you tried in Cyrenaica to nail the blue and white flag of Palestine with its Star of David over your barracks, you were punished for it. You did KP.

You didn't mind too much the sun and the sand, the sand-laden food and the loneliness of the desert. You bore the torments of the flies, the mud of Italy, the cold of the winter campaign in France. You fought in a good cause. The Nazis, the most violent and ablest of your enemies in a long history of enemies, were being beaten. For a time it didn't look as though they were going to be beaten, but you never lost your faith. You believed, also, that by fighting you would contribute to the establishment of your people's claim to sovereignty.

"Surely," you said to yourself, "now they in London will see and understand. They will revoke the White Paper. They will give us Zion, the Promised Land."

Perhaps you were one of those parachuted into occupied European countries to make contact with your co-religionists, smuggle out refugees and participate in the resistance movements of Poland, Rumania, Hungary, Austria, Yugoslavia, Bulgaria and Greece. If you were you saw from within what was happening to your brothers and sisters in the concentration camps, the extermination factories. You saw the lethal gas trucks. But you witnessed too the amazing endurance and faith and courage of your people.

Then the war ended, you went home again to Hemdah and the babies. They were thinner than you remembered. Food had been hard to obtain. Rations. There had been little milk, almost no sugar and scarcely any meat. The Arabs, you learned with some surprise and considerable bitterness, were never put on rations. They, you were told, wouldn't understand rationing and would cause trouble.

But the war was done. Now what about those you left behind in Poland and in Central and Balkan Europe? Might they not come to Palestine now? No, they could not. There was no sign anywhere that London intended to revoke the White Paper.

On the walls in the streets of Tel Aviv and Haifa and Jerusalem you saw the posted threats of the terrorists to rise unless the White Paper were voided. You saw their appeals to join the new underground, the one against the very people in whose uniform you had fought not long ago. News came of arrests and raids by the police. Your sympathies, never on the side of the terrorists, began to be aroused. You joined them, finally, hoping they'd do nothing rash, but convinced at last that victory lay only in the power of your arms.

Yes, the Jews fought. They fought in the armies of the United Nations, alongside Protestants, Catholics and Seventh-Day Adventists. They fought in the guerrilla bands of occupied and conquered countries. They fought under the flags of their native lands and under no flags at all, and they gave the lie forever to the myth that Jews are not a belligerent people but a race of merchants and money-lenders.

Yes, they had their heroes. Remember Meyer Levin and Barney Ross? Remember Radioman Dave Goodman who got one of his two Oak Leaf Clusters and his Silver Star for helping to get MacArthur out of Corregidor? Goodman was expendable, He was last reported missing.

There were Jewish heroes in the British armed services too. There was Lieutenant M. E. Jacobs, British Royal Engineers. He was standing on the breakwater that projected into the Channel at Folkestone one day early in the war. A Nazi had just been sent down in flames, shot out of the bright English sky by a Spitfire. Jacobs watched the enemy plane strike the Channel's unfriendly, heaving surface some three hundred yards from where he stood. He saw a figure emerge from the wreckage and heard it shout for help. Jacobs swam to the Nazi, pulled him safely ashore.

Why did he risk his Jewish life to save a Nazi?

"Well," said Jacobs, "I could hardly have allowed the fellow to drown."

For several weeks preceding the historic American raid on Ploésti's oil fields on August 1, 1943, one of the busiest of the intelligence officers at work planning the attack and mapping out which refineries and installations the B-24's should hit, was a quiet, unassuming and handsome British officer named Walter Leslie Forster, Major. In November, 1942, he was decorated for "courage, skill and perseverance" in preventing sizable quanties of stored oil from being captured and used by the Japs in Burma.

Also a Jew was Brigadier-General H. F. Kisch, chief engineer of the Eighth Army, twice decorated in the last war and once in this one, who was killed while personally superintending the removal of the last batch of land mines after General Montgomery broke Marshal Rommel's Mareth Line.

And there was David Lazarus, seventeen then, the youngest member in Britain's Home Guard. He was on his way to duty in London when a bomb hit a tenement house as he passed. He fought through the debris and rescued four persons. A wall collapsed and buried him as he tried to save his fifth. David was badly hurt, but he lived to receive the George Medal.

Jewish work battalions went to France armed only with picks and shovels, and those who survived Dunkerque returned to England among the best-armed troops. They got their weapons from the Germans they killed with hastily issued grenades and in hand-to-hand combat.

And then there is the story of Hannah Szenesh. Hannah was born in Hungary and went as a child to Palestine. Here she grew to beautiful and vigorous womanhood on a settlement near the coast. When war came to Palestine she was twenty-four years old with luminous blue eyes and a cloud of dark hair.

She wanted to do something about the war. She volunteered for special service in Hungary and enrolled for training as a parachutist. The British officers who taught her how to jump fell in love with her to a man and they were sad to see her go, finally, in the early part of 1944. Hannah was assigned to a particularly dangerous mission: she was to be parachuted into Yugoslavia and from there to make her way overland into her native country.

In Hungary Hannah was to make contact with Jewish members of the Hungarian resistance movement, relay certain Allied Command instructions to them and try to extricate a number of Jewish refugees from the Nazis' concentration camps and smuggle them out via the underground.

Hannah was a poet. Just before she crossed the frontier from Yugoslavia into Hungary she sent a poetic message back to the headquarters of the Jewish Agency in Jerusalem. It contained a foreboding of death. It said:

Glory to the match consumed while kindling the flame,
Glory to the flame alight in the secret places of the heart,
Glory to the heart stilled in its beat with pride,
Glory to the match consumed while kindling the flame.

Hannah was caught in Hungary and sentenced to death. She requested an appeal and it was denied to her.

A jailer informed her, however, that Hannah could ask for clemency.

"No," replied the girl, "I would not ask for clemency from murderers."

Hannah's match was subsequently extinguished by a firing squad.

Thus the Jews not only dispelled the myth of their aversion to battle, but in so doing reached a momentous era in their history. For the first time since they fought the Romans, the Jews, all of them, fought on the same side. This wasn't true in the last war. They fought on the side of the Allies and, with equal patriotism, on the side of the Kaiser. But their achievements in this war compel new respect and admiration far beyond the kudos that civilization finds itself obliged to pay Jewry's scientists and musicians and comedians.

They stand, in spite of Fascist efforts to obliterate them, at the gates of the Promised Land, with drastically reduced ranks but with a stronger claim to nationhood than ever before.

The Jewish war effort was as tangible as the muzzle of a gun, as easily measurable as the contents of a box. You can begin with Palestine itself.

Probably the biggest single Jewish contribution to the United Nations war effort was industrial. The total Palestinian industrial output for 1943 was valued at 120 million dollars, nearly half of which was strictly military supplies ordered by the British army. The industrial output six years before was worth only forty million dollars, and for 1940 sixty millions.

Workers engaged in industry increased from 30,000 in 1937 to 50,000 by the end of 1942, and the trend continued upward until the end of the war. The value of Jewish investments rose to nearly 500 million dollars. The creation of war industries, or conversion of peacetime industries to war work, was undertaken entirely by Jewish Palestinian capital without outside help.

The high degree of mechanical aptitude of Jewish workers makes Palestine the only place between Britain and India where industry exists on a European standard. Until the Mediterranean was cleared of the enemy, Palestine was the only place where expert repairs to weapons and particularly to precision instruments of all kinds, could be made in the Middle East.

Almost overnight the Jews created 432 new industries and began the large-scale manufacture of chemicals, drugs, serums, lenses, optical instruments, textiles, armor plate, shoes, heavy harbor equipment, rifle and machine-gun parts, and canned goods. A four-million-dollar-a-year industry was alone represented by the production of diamond dust by refugee craftsmen from Belgium. Almost the entire output went to the United States for precision grinding.

Within the limits of its manpower and raw-material resources, Palestine became the arsenal of democracy in the Middle East, employing about seventy-five thousand workers, twenty-five thousand of them in military camps and on port operations. A total of one-third the adult Jewish population was engaged directly in war industry. The rest were indirectly employed in helping to win the war by growing food and keeping transport moving. Palestine's production of small arms and ammunition was proportionately as high as Canada's.

The country's industrial future, however, is not bright. Many products now made in Palestine, from aspirin to jams and from textiles to shoes, offer competition to foreign commercial interests. The Palestinian Jews therefore face industrial demobilization for their wartime pains.

The British government has decided that only those industries will be permitted to continue which can obtain their raw materials within Palestine itself. And there you have another potential source of conflict between Jews and Britons. Industry means jobs and jobs mean bread and for bread men fight.

The Palestinian, and predominantly Jewish, war effort can also be measured in terms of the thousands of tons of food raised to feed large armies of Britons, Americans and even Poles who were bivouacked in and about Palestine for nearly four years. The Jews themselves went meatless, eggless, potatoless and sugarless long before rationing hit the United States. The Arabs weren't rationed, as the reader knows. The official reason: They couldn't read ration cards and the whole idea was too complicated for them anyway. The real reason: The Arab world had to be appeased in every possible way.

To Palestine's invisible contribution to the war effort must be added enormous quantities of shipping saved by the creation of industries and the intensification of agriculture. The Allies were able to divert shipping—relieved of carrying supplies to Palestine—to vital military tasks in the Mediterranean area.

In this war, as in the last, the Jews of Palestine wanted to fight under their own blue and white banner. In the last war they managed to obtain this privilege. Three battalions were formed and served with honor in Egypt and Palestine under Field-Marshal Lord Edmund Allenby. They weren't so fortunate in this war. A Jewish brigade was formed only at the tail-end of the war and served as an occupation force.

After debate in the House of Commons, Jewish insistence on an independent army was overruled. The argument against creation of a Jewish army was that, in fairness to the Arabs, they, too, must be allowed to have an independent army. The Jews countered with a proposal to have a Palestinian army composed of Jews and Arabs. This was rejected, but Jews and Arabs were permitted to join the British army. Out of nearly a million Arabs, seven thousand enlisted. Of half a million Jews, more than twenty-five thousand men and women joined up. At least ten thousand recruits were raised by the personal efforts of one of Palestine's most dynamic figures, Ben Zion, who at sixty obtained special permission to join the British army.

There's no allergy to Jews in the Soviet army. At least a hundred of the Red army's top generals above the rank of brigadier were Jews. There were about 2,-500,000 Jews in Russia when the Germans attacked. There were at least 10 per cent, or 250,000, in the Soviet army. Of these 185,000 were cited by the Soviet High Command for bravery and 5,163 honored for unusual gallantry.

Using a common basis of 10 per cent as representing the portion of a population fit for military service, you arrive at some interesting results as to how many Jews fought in democracy's armies. And more pointedly, how seriously the Nazi war machine was affected by Aryan allergy to the Israelites.

There were approximately 15,500,000 Jews in the world before Hitler's pogroms began. This represented a manpower fighting potential of 1,500,000. About 8,000,000 Jews were in Poland, Rumania, Czechoslovakia, Austria, Belgium, Hungary, Germany, France, Holland, Denmark and occupied Russia at the peak of Nazi domination of Europe. Hitler could have raised, therefore, 800,000 men for his Reichswehr among the Jews and possibly more.

The Nazis' anti-Semitism, a cold-bloodedly designed policy calculated to bolster nationalism internally and to create political and economic problems within the democratic countries to which refugees fled, proved a boomerang. In a purely military sense, the "Aryan" supermen deprived themselves of a considerable stock of cannon fodder and ensured: (1) the loyal support of democracy by the Jews, and (2) resistance from Jews inside occupied countries.

When the Germans invaded Yugoslavia, that country's 68,000 Jews had a choice between registering as Israelites and being committed to concentration camps, or taking to the hills to fight as guerrillas. Some idea of how universally the Jews chose to resist can be had from the fact that six thousand fought with Tito's forces against the Germans, including a considerable number of women. Several of the Partisan high officers were Jews. Tito's communications system, including a powerful radio station which was his most important weapon in making the world realize the extent of his power, was set up by a Jewish boy parachuted into Yugoslavia loaded with equipment.

It was a similar story in Greece. Here the Germans made their most determined effort, after Poland, to exterminate all Jews. They met, however, not only the courageous defiance of the Israelites themselves, but of the Greek people. The Rosenberg Commission, specially sent down from Berlin, ordered the arrest and deportation of every Jew in Greece where two large communities, one of 15,000 and another of 50,000, existed in Athens and Salonika respectively.

When summoned to provide lists of Israelites registered by synagogues, courageous Chief Rabbi Barzilai stalled for three days, destroyed the lists and disappeared. Tens of thousands were herded into freight cars and deported to western Thrace and eastern Macedonia wearing badges of the Star of David. Other thousands were jammed into the Baron de Hirsch ghetto in Athens. But others were hidden by sympathetic Greeks and what is more important, four thousand able-bodied men escaped to the hills and fought with bands of the National Committee of Liberation.

The best-organized underground movement, however, existed in Poland. I have seen letters from some of the leaders of the Jewish underground there. One, written by the Jewish Joan of Arc, says:

For two years we have dreamed that we would be able to tell you of our life and struggles. In the last year and a half we have built up a huge system for training youth [in guerrilla fighting]. As a matter of fact, the youth movements [peacetime organizations for training young men and women for life on Palestine's collective farms] are stronger than in normal times.

With the organization of ghettos began the systematic killing of Jews. Eighty thousand were killed with poison gas in one major city. In Lodz forty thousand were segregated and are now dying of hunger and tuberculosis. The most beautiful chapter of our war against the Nazi brute is Warsaw. There we organized a defense movement within the ghetto itself and fought several actual battles. To our great sorrow, only a small number of the enemy, about eight hundred, was killed. The result, of course, was the destruction of the entire Jewish population there. The ghetto was razed. It was entered by tanks and armored cars which opened fire on the population with machine guns and light cannon. Leaders Kaplan, Perlstein, Innovitz and Broda are among the dead.

In Tarnopol, before the town was leveled, the Jews bought pistols, contraband, at from 3,000 to 4,000 zlotys each. When they couldn't buy them they dug catacombs and lived in damp darkness to emerge by night to kill Germans.

Another said:

There were clashes between Jews armed with side arms and regular German troops. Those who survived returned to the catacombs. Some people are still hiding in them. Some of our number, alas! signed up with the police force to save themselves. They have never killed fellow Jews, but they spy on us.

In Yugoslavia organized guerrilla bands engaged in sabotage and in rescuing Jews and others from the Nazis. One letter told how Jews burglarized apartments where German soldiers were billeted and obtained thirty revolvers. Thus armed, twenty men and women succeeded in making their way to a Tito Partisan band where the price of admission was "one or more weapons." Ten others were caught by the border patrol and shot.

An organization existed in one Yugoslav city to "smuggle people out through the sewer system." The sewers were also used to bring supplies out for guerrilla units in the hills.

Almost all letters I have seen spoke glowingly of how Jews managed to keep alive Zionist movements in the occupied areas, thus accomplishing the double purpose of intensifying the fight against the Nazis and preparing men, women and children for life on cooperative farms in the Promised Land. Zionism was the principal motivating spiritual force which kept the Jews in the war. When candidates for cooperatives were sufficiently well trained in agriculture, handicrafts and Hebrew, the underground smuggled them out to Palestine where they arrived for more training and waited for allotments of land on which to settle. The difficulties they overcame before they became settlers are too numerous to deal with here, but they weren't merely obstacles of transportation, faked documents, visas and permission to enter Palestine itself.

A letter from a Jew in Budapest: "To our sorrow," the letter said,

the majority of our membership were of military age. They were drafted into labor battalions. The work fell largely on the shoulders of girls. But we continue the work of education and have regular classes in socialism, Zionism, psychology, literature and agriculture. We also have regular calisthenics.

We receive information from Palestine through the Red Cross. From them we learn that our Hungarian group there has received land and planted the first seed. From a private letter we learn that already the first child has been born there. This information gives us strength.

There was a high percentage of Jews in the Czechoslovak army and in the Czech guerrilla group. When the Free French began recruiting in the Middle East, the highest response was from French Jews.

A high proportion of the Polish army's officers were Jews. A high percentage of enlistments of Jews in South Africa brought commendations from Premier Jan Christian Smuts, and the over-all war effort of Jews within the British Empire moved Winston Churchill to say, "They rendered magnificent service."

There were nearly a million Jews in the armies of the United States and the other United Nations.

Yes, the Jews fought too. They fought and they died and they had their heroes. The dead are dead. But what of the living?

"There was a strong case for a Jewish National Home in Palestine before the war. There is an irresistible case now, after the unspeakable atrocities of the cold and calculated German Nazi plan to kill all Jews in Europe." So said a resolution adopted by the British Labor party in May, 1945.

But either the Labor government is as deaf to the cries of Jewish survivors of the Nazi Belsens and Buchenwalds as was its Tory predecessor, or the Arabs have buffaloed the British into believing that they can physically prevent the creation of a Jewish or independent Palestine wherein Jews would eventually predominate. It seems incredible that the wise British can have taken this "threat" seriously.

British denial of Palestine to clamoring hundreds of thousands of Jews who fought on our side may be based on another myth—that Palestine can't hold an increased population. It is time to look into this aspect of the matter. It isn't true any more than the possibility of a Holy War is true, but the lie has been repeated so often that it is widely accepted as an axiom.

PART TWO

It is essential to examine now the claims of opponents that Palestine is a desert waste area too small to contain the masses of Jews who clamor for entry thereto, in addition to those Arabs already there and others who might wish to emigrate later.

To begin with, there is nothing sterile about a desert unless the soil has been made somehow chemically unfit, as by inundation by the sea, and even then it's possible to wash out the undesirable salts. The desert areas of Palestine are rich with the accumulated energies of centuries held in bondage only by the lack of water. Once irrigated, the deserts of Palestine spring to life. Water restores their fertility and they burgeon with wheat and barley, the vines and figs, the pomegranates and olives that Moses heard about, four thousand years ago, when he stood beyond the Jordan on the threshold of the Promised Land.

The Jews of today have proved with practical, tangible, edible and marketable results that Palestine's deserts can produce grains and fruits and vegetables in abundance. This has required hard work, but Palestinian Jews have given the word "work" new meaning and new dignity. The methods they have employed in creating a new civilization on the unfertile, although not sterile, earth of Palestine have opened the way to what

55

is probably the only sound, scientific and economically feasible solution for the agricultural rehabilitation of most of Europe.

What they have accomplished in the deserts of the Holy Land raises them to a level with the Russians in vitality. Many are of Russian origin, and many are of German, Rumanian, Lithuanian, Polish, Italian or American derivation. Physically, and in the mode of their living, the Palestinian Jews are more like Americans than like Russians. And that goes all the way down to appreciation of ice-cream sodas and cellophane packaging. In their love of freedom of action and speech and their devotion to political democracy, the Palestinian Jews even more closely resemble Americans.

The motivating force which has impelled Jews to accomplish the improbable and often what seemed the impossible in Palestine has been Zionism, a religious philosophy which politically translates Jewish desires for safety from persecution into aspirations for nationhood. It has been charged by Hebrew and other opponents of Zionism that the philosophy is basically theocratic and nationalistic, but this accusation is inaccurate and somewhat silly.

Zionism has its nationalistic overtones, but the forces at work within it are centripetal and not centrifugal. Nationalism is a natural human phenomenon. It isn't one of the more admirable or noble aspects of man's character. But it does not follow that because a man loves his country, his native soil or the soil of his ancestors, he is altogether evil. Nationalism becomes a dangerous force only in the hands of leaders who employ its emotional powers to drive men to impose one nationalism upon that of another people.

For a decade or more before 1918, the Jews looked to America as a principal refuge from the ultra-nationalisms of a Europe beginning to feel the economic pressures of an already shrinking world. They were driven out of Poland, Rumania and Hungary. They were martyred in Czarist Russia. Then, as more recently, they became the first targets of abuse on a continent gestating war. Out of their torment grew the Zionist concept of a homeland wherein they might be free to worship, work and live as free people.

The dynamic power of Zionism can be measured by Palestine's agricultural and industrial progress as well as by the self-sacrifice, industry and intelligence manifested in the construction of the Jews' cooperative or communal settlements. The settlements provide conclusive evidence of the potentialities of Palestine as an area for large-scale economic development of the country and the whole Middle East.

To bring a cooperative village into being requires the kind of pioneering spirit which built America out of the western wilderness. The Zionist methods are intelligent, scientific, and as well-calculated as the working drawings for the construction of a Willow Run. By the time a prospective homesteader reaches the slab of desert assigned to him, he is fully trained to become a useful, self-sufficient citizen. He may have been an office worker. He becomes a farmer, dairyman, soil chemist and poultryman with sideline accomplishments in carpentry, mechanics and elementary hydraulics!

Before the war some 50,000 Jewish aspirants to a

permit to settle in Palestine were constantly in training in Zionist schools in England, America and continental Europe. There they learned the principles of agriculture, husbandry and allied crafts—but it might be best to illustrate what they learned by what they have created in the desert.

A typical communal settlement is Ramat Hakovesh, just off the Tel Aviv-Haifa road. It was a blank desert containing about five hundred acres of sand. The settlers, who numbered about fifteen families, found water. They knew how and where to dig their well. They set up their tents and began intensive cultivation of the soil. They knew what seeds to plant in order to obtain a maximum return for their work. They built temporary wooden shacks to replace the tents. The first permanent building erected was a school and dormitory for children.

One of the most striking facts about the settlements is that they are producing a new race. The parents of dark, Levantine coloring raise inexplicably blond, blue-eyed children. Nobody has found an answer to this riddle. The Jews on settlements grow into fair or red-headed, sturdy people totally unlike the pallid, harassed Jews of terrorized Europe.

Landmannschaft—the grouping together of Jews of the same national origin—is discouraged in an effort to breed this new race of Jews. Even in this, Jews show a determinedly scientific approach to life.

After the Ramat Hakovesh settlers gathered their first crop, built their school, their modern barn and poultry houses, they started their own houses. In seven years they have fashioned a model town of two hundred and sixty inhabitants. They live in substantial concrete and steel homes equipped with furniture they have made themselves. They have their own doctor and veterinary. Their bakery produces all the bread the town requires and enough to supply some to Tel Aviv. They have their own trucks and repair shops. Where there was a desert, wheat and barley fields and vegetable gardens are growing. Their citrus trees bear fruit.

No one individually has money. Their capacity for work is the only basis of their wealth and the only medium of exchange—except the goods they produce—which amounts to the same thing.

Here the Jews have contributed tangible weapons which peacemakers can employ in rebuilding Europe and in giving its peoples a new purpose in life. Jews have shown in Palestine that the forces of nationalism can be turned inwardly to benefit nations rather than outwardly in wars.

Ramat Hakovesh, incidentally, was badly damaged by British Indian troops sent to the town ostensibly to search for hidden arms, actually in as foolish an act of colonial police work as was ever perpetrated in Palestine's history. There were no caches of arms in Ramat Hakovesh, only the small arms allowed them by the law for protection against Arab marauders. It was an ill-inspired act of oppression on the part of the British to have raided a town for a half-dozen rifles and a few revolvers. The Jews repaired the village but the British never rebuilt the animosities created by their action.

Deforestation is principally responsible for the desert character of most of Palestine and, for that matter, most of the Middle East and North Africa. The forests of

Biblical days have been cut for fuel and wantonly destroyed by Arabs and others who have swept over the countryside from the easternmost crescent of the Mediterranean across the lands of Araby and North Africa to the bright blue Atlantic on the west. Subsequently the land eroded, its streams dried and became coarse waddies; but long ago this whole area, Palestine included, was the granary of what was then the civilized world. Toil and money and courage can restore it to what it once was.

Anyone who wants proof of the Palestine desert's fecundity need only travel by car from Gaza along the coast road to Tel Aviv, thence to Haifa and from there back, taking the inland road to Jerusalem, or you may go from Jericho to Tiberias, to see it. In the north and all along the coast you may see vast citrus groves. In normal times Palestine exports annually 15,000,000 crates of oranges, grapefruit and lemons. In the northern region there are large areas of wheat and barley. There is rye on the plains of Sharon and in the valley of Esdraelon. The land supports herds of cattle and sheep, poultry and goats.

A Tennessee Valley Authority project across the Jordan would make of Palestine an area as lush and fertile, as green and life-giving as the Nile Valley itself, with the difference that it would be tilled by skilled, scientific farmers, by Jews and Arabs trained by Jews. The effect of the creation, or regeneration, of such a country upon the economy of the Middle East would be of tremendous importance—but we will discuss this aspect of the question later.

Where the Arabs despoiled the forests and did nothing to restore them, the Jews have embarked upon a small but costly program of reforestation, designed as much to prevent further erosion and to raise a lumber crop eventually as to help dry up the marshes and so rid the land of the malarial mosquito.

Yes, Palestine is small—about 10,429 square miles in area, or a little larger than Vermont. It is 1/38th the size of Egypt, 1/17th that of Iraq, about 1/8th that of Syria and Lebanon, and only 1/100th the size of Saudi Arabia. It maintains easily its present population—1,697,869—of whom the Moslems number 1,042,056, the Jews 509,184, Christians 132,843 and others 13,706. But, according to eminent agronomists like Dr. Walter Clay Lowdermilk, Palestine, with full development of the Jordan Valley, could absorb 4,000,000 Jewish refugees in addition to those who are now in Palestine plus all Arabs already in the region.

Besides European Jewish survivors, only the Jews in the Arab lands are in urgent need of a haven. Since their combined numbers would not reach the 3,000,000 mark, there is, as Winston Churchill himself stated to press representatives during the Cairo Conference, "plenty of room for all—for Jew and for Arab."

Geographically, Palestine is located between the Mediterranean and the River Jordan and bounded on the north by Lebanon and Syria, on the east by Transjordania and on the south by the Sinai Desert, adjacent to Egypt. It is an unhappy enclave in an unhappy, turbulent region known as the Middle East. Neighboring Transjordania is a large but sparsely populated land, potentially as rich as Palestine.

Approximately 300,000 Bedouins and wandering

Arabs rattle about in Transjordania, which has a total population of 300,000 of whom 260,000 are Mohammedans, 30,000 Arab Christians and 10,000 Circassians. It covers an area 34,740 square miles and could easily be joined to Palestine to create a new and progressive state in a region which is falling to neglect and indescribable poverty.

At the moment Transjordania is an Arab state, set up within the Palestine mandate, although separate from Palestine since September 1, 1922. The inclusion of Transjordania in the creation of an independent Palestine should be a natural and obvious goal of any plan intended to resolve the critical situation presented by the surplus of Jewish humanity created by man's bigotry and Nazi techniques.

The Middle East, including Palestine and Transjordania, loomed large in Hitler's and his Junkers' Berlin-to-Bagdad dream. In both lands the Huns found friends among the Moslems, the most useful having been Haj Amin El Husseini—once the Grand Mufti of Jerusalem —whom George Creel calls a "perjured, crafty, evil old man." For fifteen years he incited so-called "Holy Wars" against the British and the Jews.

In World War II the mufti fled to Berlin, became a tool of Goebbels. He is the Number One War Criminal of the Moslem world and as we write he is in a suburban Paris villa, well-guarded, well-treated and ready, if the British let him, to return to Palestine. But unfortunately for the mufti he organized a Moslem brigade to operate in Yugoslavia against Marshal Tito's Partisans. Yugoslavia has a substantial number of Moslem citizens. Tito has the mufti on his list of war criminals and at last

reports, has blocked efforts to release the fellow instituted by some of his followers and friends in the Middle
East.

Whatever arguments might be presented on behalf of
the Moslems for their retention of Transjordania as an
independent Arab state—whose sovereignty is largely
fictitious in any case—must be weighed against the wartime performance of men like El Husseini. The addition of Transjordania to Palestine would provide a
sizable area of 55,169 square miles, roughly equal to
Arkansas, Florida or Illinois, and a region large enough
to house not only Europe's stateless and homeless Jews
but all of the Jews in the world if they wished. Properly
developed, the region could provide land and work for
a substantial part of the Middle East's Arabs as well.

Statistics are seldom conclusive, but a few comparative
figures will help you form an idea of the potentialities
of Palestine-Transjordania as a nation. If only as thickly
populated as England, to which the area is comparable
in size, it could hold all of 32,933,355 souls. This of
course would be overpopulation and uneconomic. The
problem is not to find a homeland for some 33,000,000
persons but for somewhat less than 2,000,000 and possibly never more than 4,000,000. You might see the point
more clearly by considering that Massachusetts, with an
area of only 8,266 square miles, has a population of
4,313,000. Were Palestine as heavily populated as Massachusetts it would contain a population of 23,402,730.
Were it merely as densely settled as New Jersey, which
cannot be considered an over-populated state, Palestine
could support 22,864,530 people.

Of Palestine's own 10,429 square miles the Jews occupy, however, only a small portion. They actually own but 6.4 per cent of the land—which they bought from Arab landowners and paid for in gold, the only money Arabs really understand and cherish. Approximately 120,000 acres, or more than one-fourth of all the land owned by Jews, is swamp land which has been drained or is in the process of draining. Jewish settlers did all of the physical work, Jewish capital paid the bills and Jewish lives often were sacrificed in defense of the miserable acres. Much good arable land owned by Arabs lies fallow or is only partially and inexpertly cultivated.

Before World War I and before Palestine was opened to the Jews, agriculture, although extensive, was extremely primitive. Arabs used wooden plows, rarely fertilized the soil with manure, hand-sowed the crops and harvested the grain by scattering it on the village threshing floor and leading cattle about upon it. Not until the Jews came were tractors, horse-drawn metal plows, threshing machines, chemical fertilization and other modern equipment and methods introduced. High prices put on the acreage by the profiteering Arabs prevented the Jews from acquiring much land, but they managed to buy enough to have established, by 1922, seventy-five settlements with a population of 14,782. By the end of 1944 the number of settlements had grown to more than three hundred with a population of 142,400. There has been little progress in this direction since.

There are three types of Jewish settlements:

1. *Communal.* In these the land belongs mostly to the Jewish National Fund and other colonization societies. Production and consumption are accomplished in

a communal way, on a cooperative basis. The organizer
assigns the people to the work; meals are taken in the
communal dining-room, clothes supplied by the communal storehouse, and children cared for in cooperative
nurseries.

2. *Smallholder settlements*. The land belongs to the
Jewish National Fund and the settler uses it under a
long-term lease. Buildings, machinery, cattle and tools
are privately owned by the settlers. Produce is marketed
on a cooperative basis, while the proceeds are divided
among the settlers in accordance with the quantity of
their produce. This system is almost identical with the
one inaugurated in Puerto Rico by Señor Munoz Marin,
the Liberal party leader and president of the Senate.

3. *Privately owned homesteads*. On these the land,
as well as buildings, machinery, cattle and accessories
are the private property of each individual settler.

To provide sufficient numbers of trained workers for
their farms, the Jews have established five agricultural
schools in addition to a well-staffed Department of Agriculture at the Hebrew University. There is also an Arab
school. This is known as the Kadouri Agricultural
School and was established with a legacy left by a Mr.
Kadouri who was an Indian Jew.

A footnote to the struggle the Jews have had to acquire land may be found in this striking fact: only a
few small areas of arable land were given free, or at a
nominal cost, to Jewish settlers by the British government. But in 1921 the government transferred to the
Arabs 235,000 dunams (roughly 59,000 acres) in the
Beisan region with adequate water supplies.

This, however, is a minor source of Hebrew discontent. There are other and far more serious ones—as when members of the British armed forces carry out punitive raids, often without provocation, against Jewish settlements. In the process not only are Jews killed, wounded or arrested but crops are damaged and the work of a season or a year must be redone.

The Arab farmer and a Jewish farmer normally work in adjacent fields and sometimes in adjacent rows without friction. One is neither friendly nor unfriendly to the other, although in the cities there is at times something resembling cordiality between Arabs and Jews. This is not as widespread as it might be. Nevertheless, the two do not automatically assail one another with clubs at the slightest annoyance, as is widely supposed. Only in times of stress such as Palestine knows now does animosity result in bloodshed.

The impact of Jewish initiative and progressive methods has shaken the feudal structure of the native Arab society, which is giving way to new standards not only in agriculture but in industry and business as well. There are today in Palestine a number of Arab banks, workshops and factories. But the greatest change has come about in and through the agricultural revolution which the Jews have wrought in the land. Arabs, by the sale of land to Jews, have largely liquidated their debts and have thus been enabled to invest large sums in farm holdings and urban properties. The Arabs now own about ten per cent of all the tractors in the country.

A look backward into the early days of modern Jewish colonization in Palestine and the progress made since gives one a clue not only to Hebrew industry but to the absorptive capacity of the country. Colonization began in 1870 when the first agricultural school was established in Mikveh Israel. In the following seventy years the Jewish population grew from 25,000 to its present figure of more than 580,000. From the experience in colonization gained by the Jewish settlers and from scientific investigations made by economic experts of the Jewish Agency, it is possible to estimate more accurately than has been indicated in general terms the extent of expansion possible in the country.

There are some 3,175,000 acres of land contained in the hill country and plains of Palestine proper, excluding Transjordania, presently occupied by Jews and Arabs. The rest of the country covers an approximately equal area of arid soil, for the moment considered unfarmable. West of the Jordan the water area of the Dead Sea and the Lake of Galilee comprises some 175,-000 acres and the wilderness of Judea an additional 250,000 acres, making a total of 6,775,000 for the whole of Palestine between the Jordan and the Mediterranean.

The Arabs occupy more than half of the land in the plains and the hills, while the Jews have barely one-tenth. The methods introduced by the Jews have enormously increased the sustaining capacity of the arable area. Originally, approximately sixty-five acres were necessary to sustain a settler and his family. Modern techniques introduced by the Jews have brought the minimum requirement down to twenty-five acres in unirrigated land, roughly thirteen acres in the richer hill country and as little as five acres in well-irrigated regions. This would indicate not only the ingenuity of the settlers but also the fertility of the soil. In most regions in the Palestinian climate, which remarkably resembles that of California, two crops and more a year are possible.

Soil experts who have investigated the situation estimate that an additional 900,000 acres can be immediately prepared by irrigation and fertilization to accommodate from 90,000 to 120,000 more agricultural families without displacing a single established settler. At least another 500,000 to 600,000 acres of fallow hill land can be made suitable for about 50,000 other families.

Jewish settlers discovered, in investigating irrigation possibilities in the so-called arid country, that water may be had by boring artesian wells, or by building dams to accumulate the water flowing from the southern slopes of the hills of Judea, or by canalizing it down from the northern rivers.

So optimistic was even the determined anti-Zionist Sir John Hope Simpson of the possibilities of expanding Jewish agriculture that when he investigated the situation in 1930 he was moved to state: "Given the possibilities of irrigation there is practically an inexhaustible supply of cultivable land..." in the presumably irretrievable desert known as the Negeb.

Even excluding Transjordania, therefore, it is obvious that, at a most conservative estimate, there is room right now in Palestine for 120,000 families or 600,000 individuals in agricultural settlements on already tillable land. By opening up the Negeb to agriculture it would be possible to settle at least another 50,000 families on new farms.

For every family put on the land at least three more can be established in industrial, professional and urban occupations. For this, as we shall see, there is ample evidence. Palestine has been endowed with sufficient natural resources to make industry possible. In any case it should be clear that from 2,500,000 to 3,000,000 Jewish people can be given a home in the Holy Land. The absorptive capacity of Palestine is limited only by raw material resources, the extent of its arable regions, the power of supply, opportunities for developing industry and commerce and transportation and, lastly, by the amount of capital available for investment. All of these, it has been shown, are in ample supply—while the people are animated by the unquenchable spark of Zionism, an important "raw material" in itself.

Dr. Lowdermilk, who spent ten weeks in 1939 studying the use of the land on behalf of the Soil Conservation Service of the United States Department of Agriculture, found evidences of the existence of a dense population in the Negeb in the Roman and Byzantine periods. The ancients had apparently developed means of water and soil conservation.

In the Bethshan plain there are thirty-two springs whose combined flow would irrigate 25,000 acres throughout the year, and the climate is such as to permit farming every month in the year. Dr. Lowdermilk predicted enchanting possibilities for the intensive cultivation and productivity of this now unused area whereon a considerable population could be supported.

In some areas the problem is not one of irrigation but of the simple hydraulics of drainage. The Huleh plain in northern Palestine is an example of the possibilities offered for land reclamation and controlled irrigation. In 1934 the Palestine Land Development Company bought 14,235 acres of this malarious region for approximately $1,000,000 and began reclaiming it. There were about five thousand Arab settlers on the land as tenants of absentee landlords. When the reclamation is completed about four thousand acres will be given free to the Arab settlers and the drainage project will benefit a total of some 25,000 acres, of which a third will be Jewish land and two-thirds Arab.

Similarly almost infinite opportunity for agricultural expansion by the application of simple engineering techniques is offered by the valley of the Jordan. An American expert, Mr. F. Julius Fohs, who conducted hydrographic surveys over a period of years, found sufficient water resources for the irrigation of enough land in the plains to make room for at least 100,000 agricultural families. The valley of the Jordan could be a Palestinian Imperial Valley.

It seems incredible that Jews still wander destitute among the rubble of Europe's civilization while the Negeb is an unpeopled waste of a few villages, inhabited by semi-Bedouins, where once there were cities like Kurnub, Subeita and Abda, metropolises of Byzantium. The remains of their drains and terraces are still discernible. Here Zion might live.

It should be at least reasonably obvious from the foregoing that what would be good for the Jew would be meat too for the Arab. The Jews themselves by their tolerance of their Arab brothers as coinhabitants of the land have shown that peace between them is as possible as it is desirable.

A fuller description of Arab-Jewish social relations

may be found in following chapters, but it can be stated now almost as an axiom that seldom if ever does the Jew strike the first blow. When the Jew has fought it has been with rare exception in self-defense, to save himself and the sacred trust of stewardship imposed by Zion.

The time for passivity may well have ended for the Jew but if so, it will be because of forces beyond his control—and, to the everlasting discredit of otherwise decent people abroad, those forces seem irresistible. The Jew has no reason to fight except as a last resort in the attainment of his sovereignty as an individual. He would much rather employ his energies in reclaiming the land from the desert and the unharnessed rivers, in rearing new towns and cities, and in extracting from the subsoil and even the Dead Sea the wealth of Palestine, the oh-so-Promised Land.

CHAPTER V: *PEOPLE*

When the first Arab landlord sold the first acre of Palestinian earth to a Hebrew settler, the Moslem accepted the Jew's presence in the eyes of the law—Arab law or any law. The process was repeated many times. Each deed transferring property rights from Arab to Jew, one upon the other, hundred upon hundred, thousand upon thousand, has created an undeniable Jewish legal equity in Palestine which no Arab, though he be a king, can deny.

The process of buying and selling was repeated often —and naturally without compulsion upon the Arab to sell the land. He did so willingly, in fact, eagerly. He sold many acres, pocketed much gold. Were it true, as Moslem leaders claim, that Arab attachment to the soil is everlasting and rises above all other considerations, the commerce in acreage would not have occurred—at least not to the extent which has put roughly six per cent of all of the area of Palestine and about ten per cent of the country's tillable land into Jewish hands.

Did the Arab perhaps hold gold above spiritual or moral principles? The temptation to say that the Arab did is very strong, but in the interest of "objectivity" it is more useful to inspect the results of the commercial intercourse between Arab landlords and Jewish peasants rather than what motivated the Moslem sellers. No mat-

72

ter what the motive, the results would have been the same.

In buying and selling land, Arabs and Jews behaved like people anywhere, and between them other commerce grew and they prospered; together, though in different degrees, they have contributed much to the building of the new Palestine. There is no evidence of what His Majesty King Ibn Saud of Saudi Arabia, in his letter to President Franklin D. Roosevelt, chose to call the "vile work" of the Jew. Rather there is evidence that the Jewish people have promoted the welfare of the Arab people in measurable degree.

There is, for instance, the eloquent although coldly statistical matter of demography. Before World War I—which is to say, before Palestine was mandated to the British after its conquest from the Turks and before Jews were admitted in any numbers—there were only 450,000 Moslems in the country. There were 55,000 Jews. By the time World War II broke out there were nearly 930,000 Moslems and 445,000 Jews. The Arabs had multiplied at great pace and there are now nearly 1,200,000. The Jewish population is still well under 600,000.

It should be obvious from this that the Arabs have multiplied at a rapid rate whereas most of the increment in Jewish population was due to immigration.

In exploring this facet of the situation, one discovers that the Moslem birth-rate increased steadily from 50.1 per thousand in 1922 when the Jews came to Palestine in any large numbers to 52.4 per thousand in 1943. The Arab death-rate decreased from 26.8 per thousand to 19.0. They have enjoyed a natural increase in population at the rate of 33.4 per thousand in the past several years.

The Jewish statistics afford an interesting comparison. Whereas the Jewish birth-rate was 34.8 per thousand in 1922, it has dropped to 29.0. There has been a sharp decrease in the death-rate too, from 13.6 to 7.7, while their natural increase has remained fairly steady at about 21.3.

The increase in the Moslem birth-rate and the decrease in the death-rate can be explained only by the introduction in Palestine of good schools, wherein the rudiments of hygiene are taught, and by the installation of good water-supply and modern sewage systems. The sharp decline in the Jewish birth-rate is further proof of a steadily improving economic condition in the country, for it has been shown time and again that birth curves decline as countries prosper. The small increase in the birth-rate of the Moslems and the comparatively large decrease in the death-rate would seem to bear out the theory.

Prior to Jewish admission to Palestine, Arab population figures showed a high incidence of infant mortality and an excess, in some regions, of deaths over births to the extent that the population was either stationary or regressing. The demographic curves provide a rebuttal to his Desert Majesty's unfortunate use of the phrase "vile work." These statistics can mean only that the Arabs, living in a civilized society, can hold their own in any population race with the "intruder."

This is particularly so in view of the fact that institutions founded with Jewish funds primarily to serve Hebrews, also serve Arabs. Hadassah treats Arab patients at the Tuberculosis Hospital at Safad, and the Radiology Institute in Jerusalem admits Arab peasants in the clinics of its Rural Sick Benefit Fund. Jewish institutions do infant welfare work among Arab mothers.

Even Mr. Malcolm MacDonald, then British Secretary of State for the Colonies, in a House of Commons debate on November 24, 1938, was obliged to admit the advantages to the Arabs of the presence of Jews.

> The Arabs cannot say that the Jews are driving them out of their country [MacDonald declared]. If not a single Jew had come to Palestine after 1918 I believe that the Arab population of Palestine would still have been around ... 600,000 at which it had been stable under Turkish rule.
>
> It is because the Jews who have come to Palestine bring modern health services and other advances that Arab men and women who would have been dead are alive today, that Arab children who would never have drawn breath, have been born and grown strong.

Anyone who has seen and smelled an Arab village in the interior of Egypt or any other Arab land and can compare it with the relatively tidy and reasonably well-drained Arab towns of Palestine, needs no further data on this aspect of the subject.

If proof were needed of the beneficent influence of the Jewish presence, from a population standpoint, it may be had in the migration of Arabs toward Jewish urban centers. Between 1922 and 1936, the increase of the Arab population in Haifa was eighty-six per cent; in Jaffa, sixty-two per cent; and in Jerusalem, thirty-seven per cent. The populations of purely Arab towns like Nablus and Hebron increased by only seven per cent, and at Gaza there was a decrease in the same period of two per cent.

As long ago as July, 1937, the beneficial effects of Jewish culture on Arab progress in Palestine were recognized by the British Royal Commission which made an extensive survey at that time. This report, too, found the fact of the growth of the Arab population "the most striking" one in its entire observation. Some of the increment in Arab population has been due to immigration from neighboring lands, but the growth is more directly attributable to the natural increase arising from better social and economic conditions.

Those Arabs from contiguous countries came because living was easier and security fairly attainable in this more modern society. In their own lands, population figures are on the downgrade or at best barely level. There they scratch a miserable existence from a miserable earth and with the technical exception of Syria, Lebanon and Egypt, are obliged to live under feudal regimes. Even an Arab, untutored and only vaguely conscious of the richness life can offer, finds himself unhappy under the Ibn Sauds and the Shahs and the other despots and semi-despots of Araby. The wages are better in Palestine!

In cataloguing the advantages which the Arabs enjoy in Palestine, it is difficult to know what to place next after their population gains.

Thanks to better education than is available elsewhere in their native lands, many Arabs in Palestine have been able to find high-salaried posts in government service. The Arab bourgeois or *effendi* class has made substantial capital investments in industrial undertakings and in citrus plantations. At least six times more Arab land is now planted with orange and lemon groves than in 1920. These alone represent an Arab investment of $32,500,000 at prewar prices.

An unascertainable quantity of Arab capital has been put into constructing buildings which are leased or sold to Jewish and other enterprises. Although not comparable to the expansion which has occurred in Jewish industry, a recent official report stated that the number of Arab "industrial enterprises" has risen from twelve hundred before 1920 to twenty-two hundred. The Arabs make soap, bake bricks and tiles, mill flour, roll cigarettes, spin and weave cotton, quarry salt and lime, and dominate the industry which produces a confection called Turkish Delight. Arabs may be seen at all hours eating the sticky concoction of sugar, honey, almonds and dead flies, which is to Palestine and the Middle East what ice cream is to America.

Anyone who sees Palestine is impressed by its vitality, its modernity, its air of Western culture, and most striking of all by how differently the Arabs look, act and talk from their counterparts even in Egypt—the most progressive of Arab countries. These conditions derive from many factors but principally from the large import of Jewish capital, totaling some $500,000,000 in the past twenty-three years. This investment has had the same effect upon the country that water has upon a desert: because of it, directly and indirectly, Arab industry and agriculture have expanded, and the Arabs have attained an economic and social status they hold nowhere else. The employment of Arab labor in Jewish enterprises, particularly in the cities and ports, has provided work for thousands who otherwise would beg in the streets by day, and by night offer their daughters and sisters for a few millemes.

Yet, although the Arabs have prospered beyond anything attained by their brethren elsewhere, they bear only a small share of the burden of supporting the public services. Arab witnesses summoned by a Royal Commission admitted in hearings that the revenues used in financing the civil governments are largely provided by Jews. While the commission found it "impossible" to calculate how the tax burden is shared, it is significant that death, inheritance and corporation taxes, in addition to levies on a multitude of items not used by Arabs, place the burden overwhelmingly upon the Jews. At least two-thirds of the tax bill is paid by them.

Since the Jews maintain by outside subscription their own education, health, social service, agricultural schools and stations, and since the direct contribution by the government to these Jewish services is almost negligible, the benefits accruing to them from what they pay in taxes is very small. A report from Jerusalem dated March 5, 1944, stated that in the ten years since 1934, the Jewish community had contributed approximately $240,-000,000 to the government budget and in return received $4,000,000 in the same period for the needs of the Jewish community. This of course did not include those benefits the Jews derived indirectly through various public services. Nevertheless it is clear that the Jew pays heavily for the privilege of living in Palestine.

It is equally clear, however, that if allowed free expression the economic forces within the Palestinian society can produce a modern, progressive civilization wherein both peoples may live and prosper without undue stresses and strains and with ultimate benefits to all. The principal one to the Jews has been the possession of a refuge—no matter how inhospitable it has been made by British unwillingness to permit the National Home idea its fullest expression.

The emergence of Palestine as a healthy economic entity is a monument to the Jews, which the Arabs should recognize and applaud rather than revile. In Palestine an Arab industrial worker earns a daily minimum 15 per cent higher than in Egypt and 35 per cent higher than in Iraq. An Arab industrial laborer can earn a maximum wage 100 per cent higher than in Egypt and 800 per cent higher than in Iraq. An Arab farm worker earns exactly four times as much in Palestine as he does in Egypt.

In these figures may be found the reason why an estimated 60,000 to 80,000 Arabs have gone to Palestine from neighboring countries in the past twenty years. In light of the fact that 63.5 per cent of all the Moslems are agricultural workers (while only 12 per cent are engaged in industry, crafts and building trades, with the rest scattered in domestic service, business, professions and the liberal arts), it is easy to see how strong an inducement emigration to Palestine must be for the fellaheen of other countries.

We have dealt so far with the tangible improvements in the status of Arabs in the country. There are also many intangible advantages acquired by the Arabs through the years of fellowship, however attenuated by sporadic animosities. Arab women for example are gradually achieving a new status completely alien to Moslem life in other nations. Their veils are beginning to go and they enjoy a new freedom in the streets and public places of the cities. This has been due to the influence of Jewish women, who enjoy complete equality with men, socially, politically and economically. It may not be too long before Moslem women will try to have kindergartens where they may leave their children under expert care while they go to work, as the Jewish women do. Eventually—perhaps as they become more educated—they may demand the right to vote as a minority of Moslem women already are doing in Egypt, where progress has been stimulated by British and, previously, French influence.

Arabs, in other words, are behaving like people in Palestine, largely because Jews treat them like people. Both in the Palestinian civil administration and in private life Jews are as proud of their contribution to the elevation of the Arab's status as they are of their own achievements. In this attitude there is much hope for the future. It is not unreasonable to believe that such profound social consciousness may eventually pay large dividends in the promotion of Arab-Jewish relations.

As a matter of fact, not so many years ago the late King Feisal expressed real hope of Arab-Jewish cooperation for a renaissance of the Middle East. That was back in 1919 when the ideals of Woodrow Wilson still quivered in men's hearts—even Arab hearts.

Men everywhere, of all races and religions, then talked only of peace and of their desire to join together in its preservation. Feisal helped Dr. Chaim Weizmann, president of the World Zionist Organization, frame the objectives of Arab-Jewish cooperation, and issued personally a declaration of friendship wherein he confessed his faith in the ability of both peoples to live in peace for the greater good of each.

"The Arabs," said Feisal, "look with deepest sympathy on the Zionist movement. We will offer the Jews a hearty welcome. Interested parties have been enabled to make capital out of what they called our differences. I wish to give you [Dr. Weizmann] my firm conviction that these differences are not questions of principles but matters of detail and are easily dispelled by mutual good will."

The intensification of nationalism in Europe following the first outbreak of the Great War of the Twentieth Century, and the gradual disillusionment of plain people who saw the world carved into colonial and imperial spoil and watched the interplay of ambitions for selfish power, destroyed what hope there might have been for Arab-Jewish cooperation.

In a world whose members were realigning themselves for another war, it was difficult to enlist the Arabs in any plan for maintaining the peace. To the imperialists and the colonialists, the Arab lands were but pieces of wealth-yielding resources in a profit pattern. They were areas to contain bases for the defense of economic interests and from which to launch attacks upon real or imagined enemies.

The vast oil-laden Arab regions attained a new value in that era, which saw the internal combustion engine become the prime source of energy in a mechanized world. The Arabs were "divided" to be "ruled." Na-

tionalism was encouraged. Read the diaries of Lawrence
of Arabia to see how this was done, what promises were
made to enlist the feeble assistance of the soldiers of
Araby in the war against Turkey. Arab chieftains were
bought with gold to fight the Ottoman Empire and later
to grant large concessions for the exploitation of their
oil wells. The ring of Wilson's call to peace was drowned
in the clink and clatter of gold.

What degree of sovereignty and independence was
granted the Arabs—and in this they have their strongest point—was largely imaginary. It was natural that
the urge to Arab nationhood should turn eventually against the Jews who had, in the Arab mind, been
brought to Palestine by the hated British—a fact exploited to the full by those who wanted no peace in
the oil regions. Disturbances imposed the necessity for
maintaining large armed forces in the region. Without
trouble, there would be no need for them; without
armies, colonialism and imperialism could not exploit
native labor and other peoples' natural wealth.

Later the Arabs became the willing tools of Fascist and
Nazi contestants of British power in the Middle East.
From 1936 through 1938, Italian and German agents
stirred the Arabs against the Jews and in so doing dis-
turbed the British, who were obliged to increase
their garrisons. All through 1939, 1940 and 1941 the
Arabs, though largely passive except for an outbreak
in Iraq in 1941, "threatened" to interfere with oil supplies in the region. The threat was not as real as some
supposed but it was there, a constant psychological
menace which gave even foreign correspondents a severe
case of jitters in Cairo when the British retreated to

the Nile, and Egypt's capital seemed endangered. Reporters went about armed against potential Arab assassins in those days.

The Arabs to be feared were not the simple folk of the plains. The dangerous ones were the pashas and the princes who were hedging their bets against the possibility of an Axis victory. *There* was the treachery, and not among the peasants and the over-worked dockwallopers of Alexandria and Haifa. These same leaders beat their breasts about nationhood now, and piously prattle about the Atlantic Charter and the self-determination of peoples!

Had Britain and America considered the common people of the Middle East instead of their self-elected rulers, and had they clung to the principles of Wilson a quarter of a century ago, not only might we have averted the recurrence of the War of the Twentieth Century but we most certainly would have peace in the Middle East today.

And had the British fulfilled the promises of the Balfour Declaration when leaders like Feisal were willing and eager to cooperate in the regeneration of the Arab world and hospitable to the idea of the entry of Jews into Palestine, countless thousands of Jewish lives —perhaps millions—might have been saved.

It is still not too late to solve the problems of Palestine and the Middle East because they are, after all, the problems of people and of their aspirations to a better life. Surely the Arab can be made to see what the economic presence of Jews has meant to him. We went to great trouble to educate him about how evil were the Nazis and the Fascists. Would it not be possible to show the Arabs through films and pictures and other media comprehensible to them what the Jews have done in Zion? No, it would not. One is forced to the conclusion that there are powerful interests at work who do not want peace in Palestine or in the oil lands— peace which such a documentation of the Jewish contribution to Arab welfare might help to inspire.

If the desire for peace in Palestine is no greater than the desire for peace in the world as a whole, then of course there is no hope. Arab leaders are neither fools nor ignoramuses. Many of them are astute statesmen and they are well aware of the contest for power which threatens to sweep aside the Atlantic Charter, as surely as the struggle for spheres of influence and special privilege destroyed the Wilsonian peace.

In the confusion and insincerity of the Great Powers concerning their objectives it is natural that the Arabs seek to maneuver for whatever advantages they can get. There again it is unfair to blame the *masses* of Arabs. It is not they who stand to gain from any concessions made to pashas and princes, kings and would-be-kings. The *rulers* of Araby are as anxious to maintain their various despotic systems for despoiling their subjects as are the coupon-clippers to continue clipping coupons.

Arab leaders fear the dynamic evolutionary force of the Jews in Palestine as much as London's Tories and New York's money-changers fear social and economic change of any sort. The Arab moguls are afraid they will lose their source of power and wealth if they lose their hold on their serfs, and in this they are unquestionably right. They have reason to be afraid, for even the Arabs are astir with new and democratic dreams.

The Jews have one tremendous advantage over the Arabs, however. They know what they want, while the masses of plain Arabs have as yet only a very faintly discernible idea.

Their notion of what the recent war was all about, for instance, was vague—and that's a colossal understatement. We have assessed, however briefly, the Jewish contribution in the Peoples' War to preserve a world of parliaments and congresses against the Nazi-Fascist attempt to substitute for it one of gas chambers, concentration camps, closed-shop politics and secret police. What did the Arabs contribute to the preservation of democratic principles? What did the Arabs do to help men retain that system of government and those ethical concepts which alone can provide them with an atmosphere conducive to the growth of their understandable and commendable yearnings to sovereignty? Well, let us see. Once again comparisons are in order. This is what the balance sheet shows.

By the end of January, 1944, 41,000 Palestinian residents were serving with the country's regular military forces. Of these 32,069 were in the British army, 23,324 of them Jews and 8,745 Arabs. The local auxiliary police numbered 9,608, of whom 5,790 were Jews and 3,818 were Arabs.

The official *Statistical Abstract for Palestine* placed the country's population at over 1,100,000 and that of the Jews 484,408.* In other words, although the Arabs outnumbered the Jews by nearly three to one, they contributed well under one-third of the manpower for

* Jewish Agency estimates: 550,000.

the Palestinian contingent serving against the Nazi-Fascist enemy. Actually the number of Jews serving in Palestine's armed forces was considerably higher than the statistics indicate. In the fall of 1944 a Jewish brigade was formed. It contained a thousand or more Jews who were new conscripts and these must be added to the list of Hebrews who went to war from Palestine. In any event, even the official figures placed the number of Jews in the regular Palestine forces at 25,695 with an additional 5,790 in the Home Guard.

In contrast to the Jews, who were able only with great difficulty to obtain the privilege of carrying a rifle—or pick and shovel—against their tormentors, the Arabs had literally to be dragged off to the war against the Axis. Of the approximately 8,000 Arabs in service some 4,000 deserted, most of them with their weapons. A rifle is worth a fortune to an Arab, for with it he becomes a leader among the unarmed members of his tribe or is able to join bandit gangs profitably. When 300 Palestine Arabs fell into Nazi hands in Greece, 200 of them joined Hitler's forces. In an Alabama prisoner of war camp there were gathered at least 1,000 captured Arabs of the Afrika Korps.

So much for Palestine. Now what did the Arabs of other countries contribute to the defeat of Mussolini and Hitler? Syria and Iraq had to be invested by General Sir Henry Maitland Wilson's forces in the Middle East to prevent them from being handed over to the Axis. It was proved that with Arab connivance the Germans had established secret landing fields in Syria for the use of Junker bombers.

Egypt and the others remained neutral. For this, however, Arab leaders and not Arabs as a people are to be blamed. The leaders shortsightedly believed that the Axis would win the war. They wanted to be certain that they'd be on the right side, counting shrewdly upon Allied magnanimity in the event of an Axis defeat, and to be secure in the knowledge that they'd eventually be able to cash their oil chips.

The Arab nations like Saudi Arabia, Iraq and Egypt made fortunes out of the war in both legal and illegal commerce. Egypt, for instance, was able to balance its budget and to show a net surplus of 45,000,000 pounds sterling, or about $180,000,000, by the time the war ended; it possessed at least $1,000,000,000 in sterling and dollar accounts in London and New York. All of it was money earned in wartime by overcharging for a multitude of services rendered.

Those are tangible assets. There were hidden ones as well. No slide-rule can compute the millions piled up by the Arab profiteers in Egypt, Iraq, Saudi Arabia and the others in black market operations. Nor can one compute the physical improvements made in the countries by Britain and America, principally the latter, in airports, railroad construction and new roads. The facilities were needed to ensure rapid communications in the prosecution of the war, but the countries where they were made now have those installations permanently. In Iran the United States built a highway running from the Persian Gulf to the Russian frontier. America also built a railroad—one of the most expensive per mile ever constructed, for in the words of a noted British economic expert while he was in Washington trying to negotiate an American loan for a British account: "They made us pay through the nose."

The figures cited earlier on Jewish enlistments do not include the Palestinian Jews who served in the Royal Air Force, the Royal navy and special branches such as commando units and the Intelligence branch. The British fully recognized the contribution to their—and our—war effort, however. They understood the difference between Jews and Arabs in spiritual and moral approach to the task of defeating the Axis. When the Tommies had their backs to the Nile and it looked as though it might be necessary to retreat further eastward into Palestine, the British called upon the Jews and not the Arabs to help them organize a security system, to prepare defensible positions and otherwise guarantee the safety of the Allied Command in its prospected new base. GHQ of the MEF was to have moved, lock, stock and brigadiers, to new quarters in Palestine, had El Alamein and Alexandria fallen. With them would have gone Cairo.

It wasn't until after September, 1940, that the Jews were given an opportunity to join in actual combat. The British scheme at the time was to raise a Palestinian division with seven Jewish and seven Arab units. Slow Arab enlistments compelled abandonment of the plan. Some 10,000 Jews already levied went into the RAF. These provided ground personnel for Palestine airdromes. After the collapse of France, they were hurriedly transferred to Britain. An urgent request for twelve hundred mechanics and air-crew specialists was directed to the Jewish Agency. It supplied fifteen hundred.

Hundreds of Jews volunteered for supply and transport services in the Libyan desert. Several hundred others became stevedores in vital ports like Tel Aviv, undertaking work usually done by the Arabs. Many of them moved westward across North Africa to Tobruk, where alongside bomb-pocked quays Churchill watched them work and saw them sweat and was stirred to tell them:

"You are unloading history."

Perhaps they were.

In Eritrea Jews covered the left flank of the advance to Keren, cutting off the Fascists on the left of the main attacking force. In North Africa they saw action in the bitter battles of Sidi Barrani, El Sollum, Fort Capuzzo, Bardia and Tobruk. In Ethiopia they performed as guerrillas, operating in suicide squads which contributed materially to the capture of Gondar, the last Italian stronghold in that country. Its fall resulted in the surrender of the Duke of Aosta.

Palestine Jews paid a price in blood for their effort against the Axis. Among the 10,000 British troops reported "missing" in Greece and Crete there were 1,444 Palestinians, of whom 1,023 were Jews. Most of these were members of the Pioneer Corps (engineers). Several hundred fought on an obscure beach in the Peloponnesus, where a British destroyer had gone to take them off but had arrived too late. They died practically to a man.

After the formation of the Jewish Brigade, the center of Jewish military activity was Italy. A Palestine outfit was already serving in Italy in 1943, but only as a supply and transport unit. It went in at Reggio di Calabria with General Montgomery and the Eighth on September 3, 1943. The Star of David was painted on the drop-boards of its trucks. Later a company of map technicians landed with the British contingent of the Fifth Army at Salerno, and after that there were Jews in action as engineers, signal men, transport troops and other special services in most actions in the Italian campaign.

But while the exploits of units of various nationalities were publicized widely, often by specially assigned home-country correspondents (the Indian army, the Australian, New Zealand and South African armies are examples) and by their own expert press relations officers and film units, the work of the Jews was soft pedaled or ignored entirely. This, it was explained, was to avoid "inflaming the Arab-Jewish question."

The psychological approach to this matter seems to be completely cockeyed. The theory apparently was to avoid arousing the Arabs. Arousing what? Their envy for what the Jews were doing? This might merely have inspired a greater effort on the part of the Arabs. Or was the policy behind the general order to ignore the military contribution of Jews as Jews, a coldly calculated one to prevent the world from knowing how they were acquiring new stature as a people by their sacrifices on civilization's behalf? Was it not perhaps intended to prevent the documentation of their case for sovereignty as a free people?

You will recall, no doubt, the deserved praise which British generals bestowed upon Indian and other troops in the desert war. But do you remember reading anything in which General Sir Archibald Wavell, one of the greatest military commanders of the last or any war, said of the Jews that they'd performed "fine work, pre-eminently at Sidi Barrani, El Sollum, Capuzzo, Bardia and Tobruk"? Where, except perhaps in pamphlets of the Zionists or other Jewish organizations, did you hear that Brigadier Kisch, chief engineer of the Eighth Army, had helped plan the defenses of El Alamein before he lost his life in Tunisia by personally picking up a mine which he thought was too hot for one of his men to handle?

The most striking single fact of the military contribution of Palestinian Jews to the defeat of the Axis is that it was strictly voluntary. As a mandated territory Palestine's population was exempt from conscription, and the high rate of Jewish enlistments can be explained only by their intense desire to participate in the annihilation of Nazism and Fascism.

As soon as war was declared Dr. Weizmann proposed to raise a Jewish force to fight under its own flag. After much soul-searching in London, the offer was accepted in September, 1940, but a year later it was shelved on the grounds of lack of equipment. The real reason was a desire to appease the Arabs.

The growth of a Jewish fighting force was long stunted by London's insistence on numerical parity between Jewish and Arab volunteers. If this insistence on parity was intended to equalize the military burden on Jews and Arabs alike, it was a Gargantuan piece of bad logic. The Arabs outnumbered the Jews by nearly three to one. On a "parity" basis there should have been three Arabs to each Jew in the army! The effect of the policy was a delay in raising a Palestine force because of the sluggishness of Arab enlistments. Physically the policy merely delayed the efforts of the Jews to pull a full oar in the Allied boat. Morally it was an injustice to brave and unselfish people.

Immediately war broke out in September, 1939, Jewish eagerness to support the Allied cause was evidenced in the registration of volunteers for national service, which brought out the astounding total of 136,-000 individuals, including women, between the ages of eighteen and fifty. Allowing for as many as four persons to the family unit, it can readily be deduced that every male in Palestine and a substantial portion of women without family responsibilities answered the call of their Jewish leaders. During the first year of the war the British command accepted only an insignificant number of the volunteers and assigned them to shoveling dirt and truck-driving, but not to combat duty.

On June 1, 1941, Palestinian Jewry announced that enlistment was obligatory for all single men between twenty and thirty who were not the only source of support for their families. In March, 1942, the obligation was extended to married men of the same age if they had no children. In June, 1942, men and women between seventeen and thirty-two were called for military service, and between thirty-two and forty-five for Home Guard service and duty as air raid wardens and labor troops. In November of 1942 the age of military service was raised to thirty-five.

The Home Guard force, which eventually totaled 23,000, included ordinary folk who had never worn a uniform or borne arms before, as well as a large number of individuals who had served in a special defense service, antedating the war, known as the *Notrim*. Founded during the bloody years of Arab unrest to guard the Palestinian settlements, this was converted to military service at the outbreak of World War II. It served on the Syrian border during the Syrian rebellion, guarding the settlements, air-fields, harbor, railways and prison camps. At least 5,000 served in the *Notrim* by the end of 1944.

Although not actually part of the military forces, *Notrim* members and others in the Home Guard performed military services which would have required at least as many ill-spared British troops to take their place. In August, 1942, War Minister Sir James Grigg was obliged to acknowledge before parliament the service of these civilian troops. They must be added to the 30,000 to 40,000 Jewish troops who fought on Europe's fronts during the war, and along with another 50,000 men and women who served in communications, fire patrol and first aid contingents, they must be added to the number of Jews who will have to be reckoned with when the time comes for a showdown.

Such are the Jewish people of Palestine. They are purposeful and well trained. They have a cause and they will not yield it to anyone. They have much to live for and much to die for.

CHAPTER VI: *PROGRESS*

In this Progress Report, assessing in more detail than has been possible before, the material accomplishments of the Jews in Palestine in a quarter of a century, may be found what Jews have to fight and to die for.

The power which has supplied much of the motivating force in these accomplishments has been Zionism. Whatever else one may say against its theopolitical nationalism it has been, nevertheless, a powerful instrument of progress. It has not, however, been an authoritarian influence. It has not exercised, as Mohammedanism seeks to do, an autocratic power.

Many Jews, in Palestine and out, are not Zionists and yet believe in and work for a Jewish National Home in the Holy Land. Their existence and their right to a share in the country's destiny has been democratically recognized in the creation of the Jewish Agency, an administrative body composed of Zionists and non-Zionists in equal numbers, charged with the task of administering Jewish interests within the framework of British colonial government.

Before taking up our calipers to measure the pilgrims' progress in industry and commerce, transportation, health and sanitation, education and government, it is necessary to assess the natural resources of the country. Upon these depend all progress, past and future. Palestine has been regarded by the ignorant or unimaginative as a wasteland where life is difficult or impossible to sustain. We believe we have fairly well established that agriculturally, Palestine's existing and potential resources are almost limitless. There is nothing wrong with even the most desolate regions of the country that a Jordan Valley Authority project like our own Tennessee Valley Authority can't cure.

In this connection Henry A. Wallace, who doesn't share the general Washingtonian allergy to the fuller life, said on March 9, 1944:

"I hope that the day will come when in a thoroughly practical manner there will be established a Jordan Valley Authority which will bring power, which will bring irrigation, which will make the desert blossom in terms of the common man of both the Jewish and Arab peoples."

The agricultural potentialities of Palestine and the whole Middle East are, in fact, almost limitless. Let us see now whether Palestine has the natural wealth essential to a well-balanced economy. Not all Jewish and Arab workers could be absorbed by farming and allied crafts and occupations. This would mean merely a lopsided peasant economy and, while its achievement would be of immeasurable benefit to the peoples of those dreary lands, their purchasing power, standard of life and general welfare would rise materially if agricultural and industrial development proceeded side by side.

Industrial progress is largely dependent upon sources of power and raw materials. Not only Palestine but other countries in the Middle East possess such resources in great and unpublicized quantities. Egypt, to cite one case, has iron ore deposits of extraordinarily high quality, assaying in richness to a degree comparable to the Swedish. It has phosphates and other chemicals vital to agriculture. Egypt needs only capital, foreign encouragement and guidance to exploit these resources. Power could be generated from the eighty-foot waterhead of the Nile, and the river's arable margins, limited now to as little as a mile wide in some places, could be extended with proper irrigation, flood control and the abundant use of fertilizer.

Instead of being an importer of food and an exporter of cotton, Egypt could thus become an exporter of food to less fortunate African and Arabian areas and an exporter, as well, of raw and processed cotton. Egyptians could increase their now miserable standard of living, buy more goods at home and abroad, wear shoes, buy more than one galabeah per annum, send their children to school and otherwise become a civilized country.

But powerful financial interests which see Egypt— and Palestine—merely as sources of raw materials or food and as a market for usually shoddy industrial products, are against any such future for Egypt or Palestine. They are interested only in perpetuating an economy of scarcity, when actually their own future industrial welfare and the well-being of all of the peoples of the world depends so much on an economy of abundance.

Palestine was richly endowed by nature, and offers opportunities for industrialization almost as limitless as its agricultural resources. It could become an industrial core of a new Middle East. Only the will and the good faith of the outside world is needed to unleash its industrial powers—just as water is needed to liberate its agricultural wealth. Both attributes the Jews possess to an inordinate degree.

Even some of the younger Arab leaders, like King Farouk of Egypt, see the possibilities. He has often expressed to your reporter his earnest desire to "put shoes on the peoples' feet and something other than rags on their backs." But his religious prejudices and his commitments as an Arab politician preclude the possibility of any alliance between him and the Jews for the development of the Middle East.

Of the more important minerals, Palestine lacks only coal and metals. What little iron has been found is of small economic value. However, engineers employed by the Jewish Agency found natural gas on the coastal plains at 390 feet and according to their reports, this source of energy seemed abundant. On the plain south of the Dead Sea certain geological formations signal oil aplenty, and the region is already being prospected. Bitumen has been plentiful since Biblical days and floats on the surface of the sea near Engedi, with large deposits in the Wadi Mahawit and important seepages near Masada.

The most important resources include the Dead Sea deposits of potassium, bromine, and their by-products. These chemicals, by the way, are already processed in large quantities by the Palestine Potash Company and constitute one of the main exports of the country. There is room here for expansion and development.

At least 100,000,000 tons of phosphates are to be found in the area of Nebi Musa and the Jebel Karmun east of Bethlehem. These can be used almost in their natural state as cheap fertilizer.

Some 25,000,000 tons of bituminous limestone were discovered overlying rich phosphate deposits in the Judean and Samaritan hills and in the neighborhood of Safad and Tershiba. In heated retorts, the limestone yields petroleum oils and gas, leaving a valuable residue of lime carbonate and carbon. Quicklime results from further high temperatures.

Gypsum is widespread, the most important deposits being in the Ghor area south of Lake Tiberias and at Melhamia. The latter consist of a bed at least forty-five feet deep. Gypsum is invaluable in the manufacture of cement and plaster of Paris

Some 1,000,000,000 tons of rock salt, procurable at Jebel 'Usdum, is so pure that it is mined, ground and marketed without refining. Sulphur, a by-product of gypsum, is abundant nearly everywhere, and there is a sufficiency of alum.

Important mineral springs, whose waters have high therapeutic value in the treatment of rheumatism and skin diseases, are found at Ain Maleh, Al-Hamma and around the Dead Sea. A Jewish concessionaire has developed the springs at Tiberias into a modern resort which can become the winter spa of the Near East.

Because of its strategic location close to sources of raw materials, such as cotton from Egypt, oil from neighboring Iraq and copper and other metals from Turkey, Palestine's industrial possibilities are greater than one might suppose even from the foregoing indication of resources. The limits of Palestine industrial activity are bounded only by (1) sufficiency of capital,

(2) the availability of technical experts and trained labor, and (3) domestic and foreign markets. Actually it either has or can supply the first two prerequisites for industrialization. The markets must be developed, but they are there—all around Palestine and just across the Mediterranean where at least one nation, Italy, has been eliminated for some time to come as a major Mediterranean industrial nation.

In any event, access to a supply of raw materials and fuel is no longer a major bar to industrialization, thanks to cheap seaborne transportation of which there is, or there should be, an over-abundance as a result of the war. American shipping has increased, for example, from about 11,000,000 to 50,000,000 tons in the past six years.

Britain has no cotton, but it is one of the great cotton spinning, weaving and processing countries of the world. Japan was, before the war, another example of a nation far from sources of supply but nevertheless an important industrial center. Industrialization is possible almost anywhere in a modern society even though it is not as richly supplied with a favorable climate, adequate manpower and raw materials, and access to the sea—as is Palestine.

Professor J. G. Smith of Birmingham University, one of the great industrial economists of our time, remarked on this aspect of modern industrial philosophy in a book called *Economic Nationalism and International Trade.*

Standardization of processes and output [he wrote], development of intricate machine tools which can be operated by comparatively unskilled labor after a brief period of training, wide distribution of electrical power and the growth of technical education in every branch of industry, enable new factories to be set up with equal prospects of success anywhere throughout the world.

Palestine, however, is not just "anywhere." It already possesses whatever minimum in the way of materials and manpower and skills is needed for industrial development. It already has a convincing balance sheet of industrial progress.

INDUSTRY AND COMMERCE

Before World War I there was practically no industry in Palestine, except for wineries in Rishon Lezion and Zichron Ya'abob and some soap factories in Nablus and Jaffa. These, together with some twelve hundred small workshops, employed no more than 5 per cent of the gainfully employed population. Today there are 1,864 Jewish factories in addition to some ten thousand small workshops employing more than 20 per cent of the Jewish population and turning out goods valued annually at $125,000,000.

The Jewish industrial establishments include factories for processing foodstuffs, metal works, machine shops, chemical plants and stone and cement factories. Others produce leather goods, clothing, woodwork, diamond dust and cut gems, textiles and fertilizers. The two principal installations are the Palestine Electric Corporation, which draws power from the waters of the Jordan, and the aforementioned Potash Company. The electric company supplies light and power to the whole country.

There are no reliable data on the development of

Arab industry, but in this field, as in agriculture, the Arabs have benefited from the presence of the Jews. In 1922 Arab investments in "industrial" enterprises totaled $3,000,000, and by 1937 the total had risen to $12,500,000. There are no more recent statistics available on the subject.

Jewish investment in industry comprises the bulk of the more than $500,000,000 which Jews have put into their enterprises in Palestine, and there is considerable additional capital on hand for expansion. During the first three years of the war (from 1940 to 1942 inclusive) money was found for the creation of 477 new factories of various kinds and for putting 133 textile shops into operation.

A distinctive feature of Jewish investment capital is that its entire proceeds remain within the country and are not paid out as interest or dividends to foreign creditors. What money has gone into the making of Palestine industry (and agriculture) was brought to the country by the immigrants themselves or supplied by Jewish national funds.

One of the best indices of industrial progress in Palestine is the increase in power consumption. In 1938 the Palestine Electrical Corporation supplied about 20,-000,000 kilowatts to its consumers. In 1939 the output was 25,500,000 and in 1940 it hit 36,000,000 kilowatts.

Just as there is no shortage of electrical power there is none in technical manpower. This has been due largely to the influx of experts from Central and Western Europe since 1933. Moreover, Jews have demonstrated a remarkable degree of mechanical aptitude.

Palestine's workers are organized in the General Federation of Jewish Labor. The G.F.J.L. has about 125,000 members. Trade unionism is spreading among the Arabs—another influence of Jewish liberalism—and they enjoy all the rights of collective bargaining, minimum-wage standards and good working conditions. In Egypt, the most advanced of the Arab nations, trade unionism is in its infancy. In Palestine it is at least in its first rompers.

Markets for the products of Palestine industry have good prospects. Demand on the home market has so far been greater than local supply. This is natural in a country which has had a comparatively large influx of immigration. Local industry, while absorbing the new-comers in its employ, has been unable to organize its resources fast enough to meet the everyday needs of a growing population. At certain periods the population, even after the influx of a large number of immigrants, was too small to warrant industrial expansion. As a result imports have been far in excess of exports.

The unfavorable trade balance is partly accounted for by the large import of investment goods, such as machinery, agricultural and transport equipment and building materials, which in 1935 amounted to 34 per cent of the total ordinary imports (not including raw materials). Comparing imports and exports over a number of years prior to recent war, the resultant trade balance is proportionately favorable for Palestine. In 1926 exports were only 22.1 per cent of imports, whereas in 1939 they amounted to 37.3 per cent. The increase in consumer imports in 1939 over 1926 was 224 per cent, while the exports increased 374 per cent.

Both home and foreign markets will expand with the

increase of population in Palestine and the Middle East and with a rise in the general standard of living. The entire Middle East, with the exception of Egypt, is underpopulated to the extent that industrial and agricultural progress is retarded. This was seen as early as 1926 by Ja'far Pasha Al Askari, then prime minister of Iraq, who said, speaking of his own country:

"What Iraq wants above everything else is more population. This is a necessary condition of progress." Similarly, Syrian economists blame their small population and its inadequate means for their nation's own lack of progress.

Greater stimulus to Palestine's industrial and agricultural development can be provided by proper government regulation and encouragement. Since the mandate was established, Palestine has served as a dumping ground for tariff-free imports which have been competing with a young local industry. The Palestine colonial administration has given no direct aid to industry, although the latter has furnished a substantial part of the administration's tax revenue.

On March 31, 1942, the Palestine government had on hand a surplus of $21,274,640, most of it money derived from Jewish enterprises. In the fiscal year ending March 31, 1943, the government revenue from local sources was almost $8,000,000 more than in the preceding year. The British government was able to reduce its subsidy for the fiscal year to $2,286,979, as compared with well over $8,000,000 provided in 1941-42.

In this substantial saving to the British treasury is contained, perhaps, the best index of all to Palestine's industrial progress.

The table below shows at a glance, however, how Jewish-owned industry has grown since 1922:

	1922.	1937	1940-41
Number of enterprises......	1,850	6,007	6,143
Number of industrial workers	4,750	27,260	45,000
Production value...........	$ 2,000,000	$36,800,360	$60,600,000
Capital invested............	$ 3,000,000	$47,013,480	$56,560,000

When war came, the existence in Palestine of an industrial organization of considerable magnitude proved to be invaluable to the Allied effort. War materials valued at more than $100,000,000 a year were produced in the country's factories. They included 3,000,000 anti-tank mines; 5,000,000 gasoline and water cans; parts for ships; quantities of foodstuffs. Some 20,000 tons of jams and marmalades for the British forces were produced, along with 7,000,000 bottles of fruit juices, 750,000 quarts of wines and 5,000,000 quarts of beer. Approximately 7,000,000 pounds of textiles used by the British Middle East forces and 1,000,000 pairs of shoes came out of Palestine factories, with a resultant enormous saving in shipping space at a time when every cubic foot of cargo room was desperately needed for the transportation of munitions and other vital supplies.

While up to the outbreak of war the majority of employed Jews worked in agricultural pursuits—thereby exploding the theory that as a group they do not gravitate toward the land—the acceleration of industrial activity occasioned by hostilities brought about a shift of Jewish labor toward factories and away from the farms. Once the country is opened to immigration, however, a shift back is anticipated.

The table below shows the quantitative and qualitative occupational distribution of employed Jews as of 1939 and 1943:

Occupation	1939		1943	
	Number	Per Cent	Number	Per Cent
Agriculture	37,000	19.3	28,000	13.2
Industry, handicrafts...........	36,000	18.7	61,000	28.8
Building and public works......	14,000	7.3	19,500	9.2
Transport, communications.....	9,000	4.7	8,000	3.8
Trade	23,000	12.0	24,000	11.3
Liberal professions.............	20,000	10.4	16,000	7.6
Clerks and civil servants......	15,200	7.9	23,000	10.8
Police and security...........	3,800	2.0	6,500	3.1
Services (domestic, etc.).........	14,000	7.3	13,000	6.1
Living on their income.........	10,000	5.2	7,000	3.3
Various	10,000	5.2	6,000	2.8
TOTAL	192,000	100.0	212,000	100.0

There are no recent statistics for the occupational distribution of Moslems, but the following table compiled in 1931 may offer a basis of comparison:

Occupation	Moslems	Christians	Other Non-Jews
Agriculture	63.5%	9.2	57.1%
Industry, crafts, building....	12.0	14.6%	12.6
Transport	5.9	25.1	6.0
Trade	8.0	7.2	8.2
Professions and liberal arts..	1.6	10.3	2.7
Public services..............	2.0	9.8	3.9
Domestic services............	2.3	15.7	3.2
Others	4.7	8.1	6.3

It can be seen from the tables cited here that there is growing in Palestine a substantial stratum of small-business men and tradesmen, both Moslem and Jewish. There are, however, no other data at hand with which to measure the growth of this merchant class. Suffice it to say that it is considerably larger than in other Arab countries. In Palestine the Moslem, like the Jew or Christian or anyone of any other religious persuasion, is entirely free to pursue the economic destiny he desires or for which he is qualified.

TRANSPORTATION

In ancient times Palestine was a western terminus of the caravan routes out of Arabia and Persia. Here were brought the riches of Damascus and Bagdad for shipment to Athens, Rome and Constantinople, or for transfer to the caravans bound for Alexandria and Cairo. Palestine was then, as now, a traffic intersection of civilization, part of the Middle Eastern bridge between the West and the Orient. The Middle East is the geographic hub of three continents, Europe, Africa and Asia, and therefore in an extremely favorable position to become one of the most important air-traffic centers of the future.

Palestine's own internal transport system, however, is decidedly second-rate. It has been developed in the past fifteen or twenty years and has been limited by official colonial antagonism to the building of new roads and the improvement of transport methods. Of Palestine's 1,586 miles of highway, for instance, only about a third are first-class macadamized roadways suitable for modern bus, truck and automobile traffic. The remainder are secondary and tertiary roads difficult to travel.

The lack of highways, like the lack of a good railroad system, is undoubtedly due to the fear of improving communications in case of "trouble." Bad roads render key centers inaccessible to farmers and others in remote regions.

Palestine's railroad system was partly-built in World War I and, although it is superior to the transportation equipment of any other Middle Eastern area, including Egypt, it is inadequate to handle the volume of passenger and commercial traffic available. All railroads are government-, which is to say, British-owned. There is one broad-gauge road 517 miles long which links with the Egyptian railway and proceeds as far north as Beirut, in Lebanon. There, if you wish to proceed to Ankara, you take a bus to Tripoli to pick up the train to the Turkish capital.

Palestine also has a narrow-gauge railway 299 miles long running from the coast into Transjordania. The total traffic carried by the railways in 1941-42 was 2,000,000 or only a fraction of the traffic borne by the buses. The inadequacy of the railway system has provided a lush field for Jewish enterprise in bus and truck operation. Practically all the passenger traffic within the country, at least as far as the Jewish population is concerned, is carried in buses and inter-community taxi services.

The bus companies are organized into cooperatives, with coordinated schedules, joint garages and repair shops, and a unified purchasing system for gasoline, tires, lubricants and spare parts. The cooperative bus and trucking companies, of which there are about a dozen, even build homes for some of their employes.

Some of the most attractive modern suburbs near the main cities of Palestine were built by members of the transport cooperatives.

Together they operate about seven hundred and fifty buses and some fourteen hundred trucks but there are a number of private enterprises too. The small trucker is not crowded out. The bus services carried an estimated 13,500,000 passengers in 1941, or approximately six-and-a-half times as many as the railroads. The quantity of freight carried is still, apparently, a "military secret." The cooperatives carried the bulk of the military traffic during the war, although many of the more prized contracts for haulage went to a British-owned trucking company which was organized with colonial administration support to compete with the Jewish cooperatives.

The cooperatives—at least one of which employs some two hundred workers and turns out bus bodies and spare parts—were an indispensable adjunct of Jewish defense against the Arabs in the 1936-1939 troubles and will be again in any new crisis.

The popular conception of the Jew as a money-merchant and shopkeeper has been expunged by his demonstrable attachment for and ability to work the soil, to rear factories, man and manage them, and to create an efficient transportation system. If the concept of a Jew as a pale-faced and slim-fingered money-changer has not already been destroyed by these evidences of his industry and malleability in a modern society, it should be by his emergence as a sailor.

True, the history of the Jews as a maritime people is recent and the evidence thereof is as yet limited, but it is incontestable. Jewish interests formed, in 1934, three shipping companies with vessels plying the Mediterranean. The ships were taken over by the British Admiralty with the outbreak of war and a number have been sunk by enemy action. The companies included the Palestine Shipping Company, Palestine Maritime Lloyd and Atid. The name of the latter company means, perhaps prophetically, "future."

In 1936 the Jewish Agency inaugurated a special maritime department, and a society known as the Nachshon was organized for the construction of vessels, training ships' crews and operating steamship lines. Three great ports were built at Haifa, Tel Aviv and Jaffa, which played a vital role in the critical supply situation existing when the Axis dominated the Mediterranean and rendered Alexandria—the only other important port on the southern littoral then in Allied hands—a dangerous one.

The Jews have also created the nucleus of a fishing fleet with some ten or twelve ships which regularly put out from Tel Aviv to fish in coastal waters. Approximately a thousand young Jews serving with the British Royal Navy as deckhands, stokers and wireless operators will provide the personnel for expansion of both the fishing fleet and the merchant marine in the months to come. A maritime school at Haifa and a sea scout Maritime Society with branches in all port and coast towns provide proof of the seriousness of Jewish intentions concerning the sea. Forward-looking leaders, mindful of the successes of small peoples in small countries like Denmark and Norway, regard the Mediterranean as a source of employment and profit both in the shipping services and in the fishing industry. Both Italy and Greece, formerly important shipping countries in the Middle Sea, have suffered irreparable losses in their mercantile marine power. There is ample room for the development of a Palestinian fleet.

The tiny merchant fleet has, by the way, its own flag. Some time ago a ship whose owners wanted to register it in Palestine and fly a Palestinian standard, put in at one of the country's ports. There existed no legal procedure for such registry. The ship remained in port for weeks until the administration provided the necessary laws. A special Palestinian maritime emblem was also designed and now flies from the masts of Palestinian ships.

Jewish merchant marine supporters visualize a fleet of about one hundred vessels manned by crews totaling about three thousand men as their immediate target in this field. They foresee the creation of a fishing fleet of about two hundred ships with perhaps two thousand crew members in the near future. Already there are signs of activity to make these dreams come true. In May, 1945, a new Jewish shipping corporation named Ziyam (merchant marine) was capitalized at $4,000,000. Almost simultaneously the Arab press reported the organization of an Arab merchant fleet by a consortium with $2,000,000 capital.

Although Palestine has three principal ports, the only deep-sea harbor is Haifa, which was completed in 1933. It is the western outlet of the oil pipeline from the Mosul fields and during the war served as a key naval base. It rivals even Alexandria, one of the world's busiest harbors, for volume of tonnage handled. Its growth,

which has meant employment for thousands of Arabs as
well as Jews, can be attributed only to the presence in
Palestine of Hebrews, as the following *peacetime* figures
show:

Port	Tonnage Entered	
	1910	*1935*
Alexandria (Egypt)..	3,698,000	6,178,000
Beirut (Lebanon)....	1,767,000	2,410,000
Haifa (Palestine)....	784,000	4,901,000

The port of Tel Aviv was built entirely by the Jews as
a port of their own during the Arab general strike of
1936. The Jews were left without any source of supply.
Funds for its construction were raised by Palestine Jews
through the Tel Aviv Port Society. It can be developed
into a major harbor. During the war it was taken over
by the British for strictly military use.

Palestine's brightest hopes in the field of transportation lie, as everyone else's, in aviation. Aside from its
strategic geographic position—one which makes it
almost certain to be a traffic junction of intercontinental
air lines—Palestine is the Holy Land of the Bible, the
capital of Christianity and derivative religions, a holy
place as much for Catholics as for Protestants and
Hebrews. It is, therefore, a travel destination *per se*.

Long before the war it was already a junction point
for the intercontinental air lines of British Imperial
Airways, Dutch K.L.M., the Italian Ala Littoria, Egypt's
Misr Airways and the Polish L.O.T. route. There were
good airport facilities and they were expanded and
improved during wartime, mostly by American Army

engineers. The prewar need for a Palestinian air service was limited, and the possibilities for employment of Jewish capital and enterprise in commercial aviation were deemed proportionately small. The Jews did, however, form the Aviron and the Netivei Avir Eretz-Israel (Palestine Airways) companies. The first has already resumed operations, and Jewish aviation authorities foresee expansion in the direction of short-haul lines running to the Lebanon, Syria, Iraq, Iran, Egypt, Cyprus, Greece and Turkey.

The opportunities for development of internal air lines are greater than one might suppose. It takes five hours to travel by road from Tel Aviv to Safed, four hours from the port to Tiberias. There is no more uncomfortable journey than the one by road from Haifa to Jericho and the Dead Sea. Planes could cover these mileages in fractions of the time required by bus or car. Communications between important centers and remote settlements could be improved.

On the whole the younger Jewish generation, thanks mostly to the war, is very air-minded, and the day is not too far off when small airports will dot the country and small planes will largely replace the automobiles and buses of today for the longer road journeys. Of this the Jews of Palestine are confident, but then their self-confidence is as heart-warming as their vitality.

EDUCATION AND HEALTH

The story of Palestine's progress in the fields of education and health since the influx of Jews can be told best by the statistical evidence. This evidence is eloquent proof of the beneficent influence of Jewry in the land, and for some of us who earn our livelihood by writing there is no more stirring parade than that of facts marching to a conclusion. First, education.

Back in 1920 there were in all Palestine only 244 public Arab schools supported by the government. The last census on education was made in 1942 and the figures show that, since the Jews have come to Palestine, the total number of Arab schools, public and private has increased to 770 with 96,928 students. In this period the population had doubled but the number of scholars had increased by nearly four times. This can mean only one thing—that Arabs are four times better off now than they were before the Jews had begun their "vile work," as Ibn Saud expressed it.

In Palestinian towns, education is enjoyed by 85 per cent of the Arab boys and 52 per cent of the girls. In the villages, where children go to work at an early age and girl babies are still drones to be sold into servitude or prostitution, education is provided for 60 per cent of the boys and only 5 per cent of the girls. Many more children apply, incidentally, than are accepted. In the towns about 55 per cent are denied admission to schools and in the villages 40 per cent. Most children attend five elementary grades in urban communities and only four in the country villages. Arab scholastic attendance would be nearly double what it is if the colonial administration provided more schools.

The desire for education is an immediate clue to improved social and economic conditions. It is probably the knowledge of this gradual uplift of the Arab masses which Arab leaders most fear, and in this fear may be found, no doubt, their detestation of the Jews who have materially helped to bring about the change in the Arab people's status. In this fact may be seen more clearly than any other the motive for Ibn Saud's insistence that the Jews be denied Palestine.

Ibn Saud's antagonism toward the Jews is comparable to that of ultra-conservatives toward social change, of the National Association of Manufacturers' brand of antagonism for the "planners" of the Roosevelt administration. The Jews are planners, architects of a good society. The Ibn Sauds want no part of a good society.

Education is the straw in the bricks with which the Jews built a Jewish society in Palestine. Although they are less than half as numerous as the Arabs, the Jews have almost as many pupils in the elementary schools alone as the Arabs have in all their institutions. In 1922 there were 15,549 Jewish pupils in 142 primary schools. Today there are 86,626 students in 751 schools.

In addition there are 27 secondary schools with a total enrollment of 4,973; 7 colleges with 878 students; a Hebrew University with 403 scholars, and a Hebrew Technical Institute with 244. There are, besides, a number of trade and agricultural schools whose enrollment is considerable, but the figures are not available.

The attendance of school-age Jewish children is compulsory and 100 per cent. Parents pay a prescriptive fee to help support the Jewish school system, while adequate social services provide for those who cannot afford it. One of the economic crosses Arab parents must bear is to see their children continue illiterate when they cannot supply the fees charged even in government institutions.

Although the Jews pay at least two-thirds of the taxes levied in Palestine by the colonial administration, they receive for Jewish schools less than one-third the amount of support provided by the government for the Arab schools. In 1940-41 the government spent $860,000 on Arab education and only $204,000 on Jewish education. In 1943 the government provided $992,000 for teaching readin', 'ritin' and 'rithmetic to roughly 96,000 Arab kids and but $300,000 to help impart the Three R's to 86,000 Jewish children. If what happened in the American colonies some hundred and seventy years ago was taxation without representation, what's going on in Palestine now is outright robbery.

But the Jews don't mind and, to their everlasting credit, don't complain publicly, officially or privately. They support their own educational system, which cost them in 1943 $3,280,000. School fees made up part of the sum and the rest was levied by local town and city councils, the National Council and the Jewish Agency.

The Jews have developed a well-integrated system of social services for the promotion of child welfare. The Vaad Leumi (Jewish National Council) which administers the educational system as well as all other internal Jewish affairs, has a special social service department for children. The Women's International Zionist Organization (W.I.Z.O.) and Hadassah, a women's organization, also work in child-welfare organizing, staffing and supporting playgrounds and recreation centers, distributing free lunches and providing special training for underprivileged or retarded children. In the rural settlements the villages have their own communal organizations.

In this field the Arabs have learned nothing from the Jews. They have no organizations for the advancement of children's social interests, still treat their offspring as chattels, to be sent into the streets to beg, to work or to steal. Some are saved by the government, which has only recently organized a social service department primarily to serve Arabs. The Jews often contribute to the aid of Arab children, particularly through the humanitarian agencies of Hadassah. Private institutions and missionaries help all they can, but on the whole the Arab child has an unhealthy, untutored present and an uncertain and unhappy future to look forward to.

The physical well-being of a country's citizens should be one of the principal responsibilities of government. In Palestine the government Department of Health has been notorious for its disregard of Jewish needs and for the inadequacy of hospital facilities for the Arabs. Government expenditures for public health have risen gradually over the past ten or fifteen years. The appropriation for 1941-42, the period of the last public statistics, totaled $1,187,640 or double the 1921-1922 expenditure, but this sum represented only about 4 per cent of the total government budget as compared to nearly 8 per cent ten years ago.

Hadassah has borne the brunt of financing the upkeep of Jewish health in Palestine with funds gathered from Jewry all over the world. In 1941-42 this one organization spent $835,080 on public health, only slightly less than the government itself laid out. In one year, 1935-36,

the cost of maintaining the Jewish health services was
$1,400,000, of which the government contributed only
3 per cent.

Tuberculosis is a common disease in the under-
nourished Middle East. Palestine, where food is usually
more abundant than in neighboring countries, doesn't
escape the scourge. The Arabs are, of course, the principal victims. In predominantly Arab Safed, Hadassah
maintains the only tuberculosis clinic. In 1941 it
registered 162 patients. Of these, 18 were Moslems.

GOVERNMENT

British control of Palestine is theoretically subject to
the supervision of the non-existent League of Nations.
The Permanent Mandates Commission of the League,
which was an independent, non-political body, censured
British administration of Palestine repeatedly. But the
commission's reports would go to the League Council
and there the criticisms were explained away by the
British representatives. Whenever a resolution on Palestine came up for a vote, Britain, through her dominant
position in the League, would always obtain approval
of her stewardship.

At this moment, even while the provision on trusteeship for dependent territories is part of the United
Nations Charter, British control of Palestine is complete, absolute and subject perhaps only to possible
censure by world public opinion.

Although British presence in Palestine is derived
from the mandate granted by the League of Nations,
the Constitution of Palestine is an Order-in-Council

issued by the British government establishing the government of Palestine. At the head of the government is the High Commissioner whose regular term of office is five years, although some stayed longer while others remained for a shorter time. The High Commissioner is also the commander-in-chief of the country.

He is, moreover, the High Commissioner of Transjordania. He has an Executive Council which has advisory power and which is composed of the Attorney-General, the Secretary-General, the Treasurer of the Palestine government and other departmental heads. The number in the Executive Council has changed many times during the last twenty-five years.

The departmental heads are colonial officials; during the first civil administration, which was initiated in July, 1920, many of the officials, department heads and others were left-overs from the military administration; they had no other qualifications for their position except that they were in the military force that occupied the country. Naturally the administration of the country suffered seriously.

The government departments embrace practically all functions of government, and in many cases even that of municipal service. For administrative as well as military reasons the country was divided into districts, varying in number from three to ten, at the head of which were governors, and sub-districts at the head of which were district officers. Most of these officials were Britishers, although some of the junior officials were "natives"—Arabs and Jews.

During the last twenty-five years the Palestine government has made some attempts to introduce central self-governing institutions, but they all failed. In 1922 the government made a serious attempt to establish a legislative council, but with very limited powers. However, the Arabs boycotted elections to the council and the government had to give it up. Another try was made in 1936, but nothing came of it.

The people have no direct voice whatsoever in the government, although an inadequate, indirect route to enable people to participate has been inaugurated. The scheme calls for the publication of new laws in the "Official Gazette" a number of weeks before they become Acts. During these weeks the people may present their opinions and arguments against the law, and if the government finds them valid, it may modify or withdraw the law completely. But this is done arbitrarily and has no legal basis whatever. Furthermore, this device does not apply to government financing and budgeting!

Jewish organization is of different types and has various functions. The Jewish Agency, representing both the World Zionist Organization and the non-Zionist Jews throughout the world interested in the upbuilding of Palestine, is the major representative of the Jewish people as far as Palestine is concerned. The Agency is *elected* by the World Zionist Organization at the latter's congress meetings, which normally meets every two years, and by the various Jewish communities throughout the world. The Agency is officially recognized in Articles 4, 6 and 11 of the mandate for Palestine.

In their own community the Jews are organized in a body known as Knesseth Israel, of which every male and female eighteen years and over is a member. The representative body of the Knesseth is the Assephath Hanivcharim (Elected Assembly), *elections* for which are held every four years and every member of the Knesseth has a right to vote. The Assephath Hanivcharim is the parliament of the Jewish community in Palestine, dealing with all internal matters affecting Jewish life, such as education, health, social services, religious institutions and the courts.

The Assephath Hanivcharim elects a Vaad Leumi (National Council), which functions when the Assephath is not in session, and the Vaad Leumi elects an executive which carries out the work of the Knesseth. The system is, in essence, a democratic application of the soviet idea.

Another important major organization of modern Jewish Palestine is the Histadruth Haovdim (General Federation of Jewish Workers in Palestine), which fulfils the function of a trade union federation and deals, in addition, with settlement, health, cultural and educational matters. It also prepares new candidates for immigration into Palestine. It is the strongest single Jewish organization in the land with an advanced program of social and economic activity.

For the Arabs political life hardly existed before 1908, when the Turkish Revolution gave a strong impetus to Arab nationalism—although it cannot be said that Palestine's Arabs had a substantial share in this. Politics meant to them only anti-mandate and anti-Zionist intransigeance. The Arabs split into small factions around the great land-owning families, whose influence was rooted in their wealth, their political power and ecclesiastical standing under the Turks. Political life was extremely personalized and ruled by cliques, especially by the Jerusalem families of the Husseinis and the Nashashibis.

The most important personage among Palestine's Arabs has been the ex-mufti of Jerusalem, the infamous Haj Amin El Husseini. The mufti held at his command a strong clan organization; he possessed governmental and ecclesiastical authority and funds acquired when the British appointed him mufti of Jerusalem (*i.e.*, authority on Moslem religious law and affairs); and he was president of the Supreme Moslem Council, a body created by Britain to supervise Moslem religious endowments and courts.

The political activity of the Arab leadership under the mandate found expression in "congresses," resolutions, memoranda, negotiations, lobbying, and in wild anti-Jewish propaganda. Throughout, these congresses have remained gatherings of politicians and agitators and have never produced an organization of rank and file membership.

The squabbles of factions and individuals aloof from the masses, without the basis of mass movement or popular organization, eventually nullified the "Arab Executive" elected by the congresses. This executive or ruling body was headed until 1934 by an older member of the Husseini family, Musa Kazim Pasha. But the real leader was always Haj Amin. His chief lieutenant was his nephew, Jamal El Husseini, deported to Rhodesia after his capture in Iran. During the troubles of 1936 the Arab notables set up a Higher Arab Committee which was broken up by the turn to violence in that year. At present there is no generally recognized higher Arab body.

From the foregoing it is clear that in the field of politics, too, the Jews have made substantial progress. Jewish organization is based on democratic principles and is subject to democratic processes and checks and balances. Arab organization, on the other hand, is still in a backward stage. Democratic processes are unknown to them and leadership is a matter of personal power derived from the strength of individual cliques, wealth and influence in the church.

Arab leaders purposefully employ the slogans and language of Western democracy—as witness Ibn Saud's professed adoration of the principles of the Atlantic Charter—but they neither understand the meanings of those slogans nor apply its precepts in everyday life.

The actual organization of Arab life in Palestine contains less democracy than Boss Hague's administration in Jersey City and even less than the Fascists' corporate state.

PART THREE

CHAPTER VII: *ALLAH*

Every day at dawn, noon and sunset the muezzins emerge upon a million minareted mosques everywhere in the Kingdom of Islam and call the Faithful to prayer. Every Mohammedan, rich or poor, kneels on his prayer rug, turns toward Mecca where Mohammed was born and prostrates himself.

The rug may be a precious Kashan woven in silk and worth a small treasure or it may be a dirty, tattered oblong of burlap. But its function is the same—to serve as an altar whereon to make the Moslem devotions. At that moment there is, between ragged beggar on burlap and the pasha on silk as they kneel and bow low, a bond stronger than any the infidels know. It has endured a thousand years through a common language and a common racial origin.

Translated into politics such unity becomes a powerful force in world affairs. The tendency of modern man everywhere has been to separate Church and State, to put religion and politics into separate compartments. In Islam, Church and State are identical. The objectives of one are the aims of the other. Having no sound political philosophy within whose framework Arabs may attain economic, social and political security, their leaders have substituted the powerful religious one.

They cannot summon their followers to struggle

toward more wages, more bread and the amenities of civilization because in so doing they would necessarily need to yield the privileges and power they now enjoy. Through religious pressures alone can Arab chieftains achieve their ends. But there are sharp differences among them which the average Westerner does not see, and he is thus deluded into believing in "Arab unity."

The Moslems have for years talked of forming an Arab federation. But because federation implies the yielding of some modicum of sovereignty to others—something which no Arab leader is willing to do—Arab unity is a fiction.

That at last such a "federation" exists is one of the strangest phenomena of the Middle East, one which students of Middle Eastern affairs find difficult to accept at face value. The nations of the region have "bound" themselves into what they call an Arab League, with common objectives along political, spiritual and cultural lines. At present the league is busy trying to form a federation of Palestine, Syria, Lebanon and Transjordania, to be known as Greater Syria.

The historic precedent for such a federation is found in the remote fact that before 1914 the entire region under the Turks was loosely described as Syria. Ibn Saud has consented to the creation of a Greater Syria, and it is the intention of the fathers of the scheme to place upon the throne of the new state the regent of Iraq, the Emir Abdul Illah. Syria and Lebanon have recently been granted their independence as free republics, or they were as this was written.

It is curious that the Arabs who have cried so long

for freedom are willing to exchange a republican form of government for a monarchical one. It is not too remarkable however when viewed against the background of British efforts to oust the French from the Levant and to develop any scheme for keeping the Jews a subject minority no matter what happens. Even if given Palestine as a state of their own, the Jews in a greater Syria would remain numerically inferior to the combined Arab populations of Syria, Lebanon, Iraq and Transjordania.

One hope for frustration of the Greater Syria scheme lies in the objections of the large majority of the Arab Christians in Lebanon known as Maronites. It has been proposed that they be left in a separate Maronite republic—a magnanimous offer on the part of the Moslems. Such magnanimity is not to be expected, of course, on behalf of the Jews. Every nerve is being strained by Arab leaders, whose eyes are fastened on the restoration of an Arab empire to rush the scheme through before any final decision is made by the Great Powers in respect to Palestine.

Religion to the Arab boot-black or beggar, clerk or servant, is a real and powerful force. To Arab leaders it is an instrument of politics and as much a bargaining counter as ownership of an oil well.

You find little of the True Faith among Arab premiers and pashas and kings. Mohammedanism prohibits, for example, the use of alcohol, particularly during religious feasts. But while the Faithful deny themselves, their leaders are among the more renowned tipplers in the whole realm of imbibers. You may find proof of this in Wendell Willkie's *One World*. In his travels through the Middle East Mr. Willkie met a number of Arab potentates who were stout drinkers, a fact well known to any number of British, American and other officials and certainly to American correspondents who have passed any time in Arab lands. The tarboosh was once a symbol of religious loyalty. Today it is merely the badge of a new and less admirable Arabism.

To the true Moslem Allah is God, and Jesus was not the Son of God but merely another prophet like Moses. To him the Bible is just a storybook, while the only true holy book is the Koran which Allah gave to Mohammed, his prophet. An Arab is an idea that walks like a man and like a man can be led into green pastures. Unfortunately, it is not the purpose of Arab leaders to lead the individual to a richer and better life, but rather to use him for their own ambitious political ends.

For these leaders corruption is a way of life, graft is a political technique; the record of their chicanery and chauvinism needs no documentation here. It can be found, among other sources, in the Black Book which records the financial machinations of a certain Egyptian Arab politician, a late premier.

In Islam—the Kingdom of the Faithful—Americans or Greeks, Britons or Armenians are tolerated only because they are strong or rich. Mohammedanism in itself is basically xenophobic. Certainly there is no place in its theocracy for the Jews. It is to life in the Middle East what Shintoism was in Japan—but like Shintoism, the Mohammedan philosophy has admixtures of good with evil: it can be an instrument of progress if properly put into its place as a religion not as an all-inclusive politico-religious philosophy.

Another reason why the vaunted Arab federation may never materialize is the competition for power among the various kings of the Arab lands. Ibn Saud would never accept anyone else as caliph of Islam.

When Egypt's young King Farouk grew a beard, for instance, he was immediately plunged into political trouble—for this was an event, in the Moslem mind, of vast importance. Farouk grew the whiskers for the excellent reason that he hates to shave; but high up in Islam's hierarchy it was taken to mean that he would look favorably upon the idea of becoming caliph of the Faithful. To Sheik Mustapha El Maraghi, Farouk's childhood tutor and a Moslem potentate, the Faroukian beard meant that Farouk wanted to be caliph of the new, united Arab world they dream about.

The title of caliph died with the Ottoman Empire. It was given to the political and religious ruler of Islam and was the Mohammedan equivalent of Holy Father, or Pope. Without a beard Farouk was simply a political figure, a king. With a beard cut, as his was, in the full, round style prescribed by the Koran, Farouk acquired the aura of a religious as well as a political ruler.

Immediately at Cairo's El Azhar, the largest and most influential Moslem university in the world, the cry went up: "Araby for the Arabs and Farouk for caliph." Outwardly, El Azhar is just another beautiful mosque. Actually, it's the epicenter of Arab nationalism, which radiates outward to every corner of the Arab world. Sheik Mustapha El Maraghi is El Azhar's rector.

Farouk doesn't want to be caliph. His name in Arabic means "one who can distinguish right from wrong." It was probably the advice of his father, Fuad, however, rather than any highly developed power of discrimination that guided Farouk away from the caliphate. Before he died, Fuad told his young son never to fall for the caliph lure—in short, to stay out of Arab religious affairs. "You will have trouble enough ruling Egypt," Fuad said, "without trying to govern all the Moslems in the world."

Fuad was a wise man. Although not a full-blooded Arab himself—he was of Albanian and French as well as Egyptian stock—he knew the Arabs. He knew how difficult it would be for Farouk to stick to politics and keep out of religious affairs in dealing with a people to whom politics and religion are synonymous. Fuad's last words contained sound advice not only for a king-to-be but also for outsiders who want to do business with Arabs—whether to negotiate a new trade treaty, an oil lease or the right-of-way for a pipe-line.

Chief of Islam's avowed aims is full independence from those foreign powers which, directly or indirectly, dominate the Arab world. The issue rises darkly to obscure relations between Britain and France, the two principal imperial powers in the Mediterranean and rivals for domination of the strategic Levant. Furthermore, it complicates relations with Russia.

The Arabs know they have something that at least Britain and the United States want—oil. Their leaders are shrewd. They will sell that oil, or the rights to pump, refine and transport it, at the highest possible rates. Their price is not merely gold. More than gold they want power.

Less than a thousand years ago, the Arabs owned an empire that lay like a fat, distorted horseshoe over

Portugal, Spain and part of France, spread across North Africa and the Middle East. If Charles the Hammer hadn't stopped them at Poitiers, they might have conquered all Europe, turned the course of civilization into Allah only knows what dark channels. This is the Arab heritage of imperial greatness.

They don't at the moment envision the reconquest of that empire. But they have definite territorial and political ambitions which cannot be fulfilled without blood-letting—or else new, large-scale appeasement to prevent it.

Right now they will settle for ejection of the Jews from Palestine or the creation there of an Arab state wherein the Jews, outnumbered as they are, would be a permanently subjugated minority. There would be no cause for trouble here if the Jews would willingly accept such arrangement, but they won't. They will fight. Nothing happens in one part of the Arab or Moslem world that doesn't have immediate repercussions in another. And the man who usually pulls the wires is not a king or even a prominent politician, but the little-known, mild man who rules El Azhar, Sheik Mustapha El Maraghi.

The political means whereby the Arabs hope to expel or subjugate the Jews in Palestine is the federation or union of all Arab states. Sheik El Maraghi, with his dream of restoration of the caliphate, is the most powerful supporter of the scheme.

His voice, for instance, was loudest in support of Lebanese independence when the first shots were fired in the new Arab fight for freedom. What happened in Lebanon was largely suppressed by British censorship for the sake of Allied unity and to prevent the Nazis from obtaining valuable propaganda material. The prelude to a bloody symphony was played unheard.

Here, briefly, are the facts: Tiny Lebanon (with a population of 1,000,000 in an area the size of Puerto Rico), which was ruled by the French under a League of Nations mandate, had elected a new parliament and president. The majority of the people, or about six hundred thousand, are Christians, mostly Maronite Catholics. The remaining four hundred thousand are Moslems of various sects. The Christians are pro-French, the Moslems aren't.

It was agreed that the Christians should have thirty seats in the parliament, and the Moslems twenty-four. On a basis of proportional representation this wasn't quite fair, but it didn't matter. The elections were about as crooked as they come. The French backed the Maronite majority, while the British supported the Arab Moslem minority, which also had the moral support of the United States. French and British gold flowed freely.

Under Lebanese law, the president is chosen by the Chamber of Deputies. The chamber named Sheik Beshara El Khoury, a fat, bald little man, intensely nationalist and anti-French. He was also the British choice. Almost his first act when he and the members of parliament took office was to declare Lebanon's independence from France. Did not the Atlantic Charter express an Anglo-American desire to see people acquire sovereignty and achieve self-government? It was a historic occasion, for it was the first test of the workability of the Roosevelt-Churchill blueprint for war and peace.

Lebanon and Syria had been freed from Vichy by British troops in 1941. They were occupied by British and Free French troops to prevent their use by Axis air forces. The Free French promised "to put an end to the regime of the mandate and declare the peoples of Lebanon and Syria free and independent"—a pledge guaranteed by the British government.

In spite of all this, however, the Lebanese knew that nothing had changed—that they had simply swapped old masters for new. When Sheik El Khoury bluntly announced Lebanon's independence, the de Gaullists clapped him and most of his deputies in jail. Senegalese hirelings patrolled the streets and French tanks sealed the Moslem quarter to keep the Arabs in check. But the Moslems broke the seal, staged bloody riots and demonstrations amid shouts of "Down with Tyranny" and "Down with Oppression."

British and American backing for the Lebanese government's move was interpreted by the French as an attempt to strip France of her empire in the Levant while she was prostrate. General Catroux, lean de Gaulle handyman in colonial affairs, said as much. The French broke a few skulls and killed a couple of people before they released El Khoury and the others and agreed to negotiate a treaty giving Lebanon independence on a basis similar to that enjoyed by Egypt—after the war. Loudest in their objections to the arrests and the settlement were the Arab Moslems.

Arab unity was proved when de Gaulle's cops pinched El Khoury. Every Arab leader in the Middle East howled with indignation. In faraway Cairo, King Farouk protested. So did Premier Nahas Pasha. So did night-gowned Arabs whom no one had suspected of any political consciousness. They swirled through Cairo's streets shouting, "Down with de Gaulle."

But of all the voices raised in protest, none carried such weight as that of Sheik Mustapha El Maraghi. The sheik is a quiet, taut little man of seventy, with an ascetic face, a noble white beard and the sparkling, restless eyes of a bird of prey. He has a well-modulated voice and an unctuous manner. To Main Street eyes, Sheik El Maraghi, in his long-sleeved, ankle-length purple silk robes worn under tight-waisted, double-breasted black broadcloth overcoats, looks as ludicrous as a man wearing a chesterfield over a nightgown. But there is nothing ludicrous about the sheik. He is one of the unfunniest men in the world.

Sheik Eli Maraghi is the Arab archpriest of nationalism and the godhead, therefore, of one of man's strongest emotions—love of country. He is the most powerful single leader of the reborn movement for Arab "independence." Nor is his influence limited to the Middle East, for the sheik is a Moslem as well as an Arab, and, as such, his influence extends into India, where a vast minority of sixty million cries epithets against the British and demands Pakistan—the division of India into separate states, including, of course, one for the Moslems.

The sheik's influence is exercised through El Azhar and is overwhelming. Almost any Arab chieftain can raise enough riflemen to attack a Jewish village or a British outpost. One or two, like King Ibn Saud of Saudi Arabia and Farouk of Egypt, can raise small armies. But El Maraghi is far more powerful than any of these. He deals not in guns but in ideas. In El Azhar, he trains the priests who preach nationalism throughout the Moslem world.

To his university in Cairo come about fifteen hundred students each year for a ten-year course in Arabic grammar, rhetoric, literature, mathematics, logic and history. They come from French and Spanish Morocco, Libya, Algeria, Tunisia, Egypt, Palestine, Lebanon, Syria, Iraq, Iran, Saudi Arabia and the Yemen. These comprise the lands of the Arab world proper. Students also come from China and India, and before the war they came from as far away as Japan and the Philippines.

If the priests' studies were limited to Koranic culture and the Mohammedan religion, the chances for permanent peace in the Middle and Far East might be rather good. But reading, writing, arithmetic and the tenets of the Koran aren't the only things the seminarists learn at El Azhar. Before them is held, for ten years, the dream of a reborn Arabia Felix—Happy Arabia—ruled and administered by Arabs for Arabs and dedicated to the greater glory of Mohammed.

Here they become imbued with the messianic spirit of Mohammed, who one morning announced to his wives that he was the voice of God on earth and thereafter based his every action on this belief. El Azhar, which for a thousand years has resisted all efforts at reform, is theologically fundamentalist and prides itself on its nationalistic politics. El Azhar hates Jews.

Arab politicians keep the Jewish issue alive out of fear. They are afraid of the Jews' prowess as farmers and craftsmen and organizers. They fear the Jews' progressiveness. They are terrorized at the possibility that the Jews, once given a homeland in Palestine, would thrive and multiply and spread into adjacent lands and eventually become the dominant economic, political and religious force in the Middle East.

The elimination of the Jews, therefore, has become the chief aim of Arab nationalism. If a student comes to El Azhar with any kindly feelings toward Jews, these sentiments are quickly eradicated in an intensive course in racialism. Islamic tenets don't include the superman nonsense of the Nazis, but since they do teach intolerance of other races and religions, the effect is the same.

The only reason the Moslems didn't constitute so great a menace as the Nazis is that they are a backward, illiterate and unindustrialized people, weakened by disease and by centuries of foreign exploitation. For four hundred years after they passed their imperial peak, they were subjected to the rule of the corrupt Ottoman Empire, whose hold wasn't completely broken until the end of the last war.

Turkey was Germany's ally in the last war, and the Arabs of Hedjaz helped to defeat the Turks while the Arabs in other lands fought with Turkey against the Allies. Sherif Hussein of Hedjaz, later "King Hussein" received in payment good gold and independence. Iraq, Transjordania and Egypt were helped on the way to their independence in partial fulfillment of British obligations.

But Great Britain was also deeply obliged to the Jewish people. There was the invention of Chaim Weizmann, which was so helpful to the Allied war effort. And there was the much wider support of world Jewry for the Allied cause at a most critical moment in

the war. The Balfour Declaration was the promissory
note issued by Britain to the Jewish people in payment
for all that.

In London on May 29, 1941, while British lives were
being sacrificed in the Western Desert to defend Egypt
and in the Levant to liberate Lebanon and Syria,
Anthony Eden made a statement that (*a*) practically
canceled the Balfour Declaration which opened Palestine to the Jews, and (*b*) gave the Arabs a basis for
more vigorous political action toward fulfilment of their
nationalist and anti-Semitic aspirations.

Eden said:

This country has a long tradition of friendship with the
Arabs. We have countless well-wishers among them, as they
have many friends here. Some days ago I said that His
Majesty's government have great sympathy with Syrian aspirations for independence. But I would go further.

Many Arab thinkers desire for the Arab peoples a greater
degree of unity than they now enjoy. In reaching out for
this unity, they hope for our support. No such appeal from
our friends should go unanswered. It seems to me both
natural and right that the cultural and economic ties between Arab countries and the political ties, too, should be
strengthened. His Majesty's government will give their full
support to any scheme that commands general approval.

Immediately El Maraghi, Saudi Arabia's King Ibn
Saud, Farouk and every other politician in the Middle
East got to work. Cairo's hotels were filled with sheiks,
pashas and princes, gathering to marshal that "general
approval" Eden talked about.

The Arabs cleverly changed their strategy from
espousing anti-Zionism to Arab federation. If they got

their federation, they could eliminate the Jews very nicely without incurring the resistance of pro-Jewish America and the liberal, idealistic elements in England.

To the assembled Arab dignitaries, Nahas Pasha, Egypt's late ambitious, wall-eyed prime minister and one of the slickest politicians in the Middle East, said: "Events are moving swiftly in the world—we must be united; otherwise, we may sink." The tentative federation plan, worked out in conferences in Cairo and Alexandria, made very certain that the Arabs would not sink. Thus, preliminary plans were laid for what will probably be Europe's biggest postwar headache.

Here is what the Arab leaders have cooked up: A big federation to include Egypt, Saudi Arabia, Iraq; a smaller federation to consist of Palestine, Lebanon, Transjordania and Syria. In such an arrangement, the half-million Jews in Palestine would be vastly outnumbered by seven million Arabs. The Jews would have little or no voice in the affairs of the Middle East.

Germany's "Colonel Lawrence," Dr. Hans Grobba, did his work well in the Middle East and, when war came, most Arab countries were more disposed to do business with Adolf than with the Allies. Ibn Saud even sent Hitler good Yemen coffee to replace the Nazis' *ersatz*. Grobba bought Rashid Ali in Iraq and he bought Hadj Amin El Husseini.

Though Britain's fear of Arab rebellions lessened after Eden's 1941 speech, appeasement of the Arabs at the Jews' expense has continued and reached a new high when Palestine was closed to Jewish immigration. There was good reason for this: The Arabs have the oil.

We shall discuss oil and its relation to the politics of the Middle East and the Palestine problem in the next chapter. Oil is the Arab chiefs' blue chip in the desperate international poker game being played out in the Middle East, and their prattle about "prior ownership" is merely a catch phrase for the unwary, the semi-literate and those predisposed to reject Jewish claims to the country. The Arabs conquered Palestine some thirteen hundred years ago, but by 1071 their rule ended and there hasn't been anything resembling an Arab government in Palestine since. In the roughly 425 years of their suzerainty in Palestine the Arabs hastened the destructive work of wind, sun and erosion. In the twenty-five years since the Balfour Declaration allowed them to do so, the Jews have repaired some of the damage. Arab claims to the Holy Land on ethnological grounds are no more valid than those based on prior possession. Roughly 75 per cent of the Arabic-speaking inhabitants of the land are recent immigrants or the descendants thereof.

But it is on political and moral grounds that the Arab case in Palestine is weakest. There is little or no relationship between the forms of Arab society and democracy as we know it—with the exception of the feeble experiments in popular government in the Lebanese and Syrian fragments of the Arab world (influenced largely by Christian rather than Moslem elements) and in Egypt, where self-government is still in its infancy. The Arab political patterns are generally more congruent to the Nazi and Fascist forms than to ours.

The bulk of the Arabs, for example, do not see a war criminal in the mufti. He is, instead, something of an

Arab hero. He merely made a mistake in backing the losers. The experience of Kemal Ataturk in attempting to westernize Turkey, in any case, provides ample evidence of the Arabs' resistance to democratization. Kemal was never able to have a free parliament. He went to the extent of creating a fictitious opposition party in an effort to teach the Turks parliamentarian procedure and the art of debate. But debates broke up into emotional quarrels and fist fights. Encountering a wall of reaction formed by the clerics, the corrupt, immoral and wealthy bourgeois classes and the feudalistic sheiks and emirs who had lorded over Turkey for centuries, Ataturk was obliged to dissolve the "opposition party." With Ataturk's death the country began to slip back into the old ways.

It will take centuries for the Arabs to emerge as a truly democratic people. The presence of a Jewish state in the Middle East would hasten that emergence. To understand how truly backward the Arab civilization is, one needs only to ride through Arab countries in a train or automobile. It is not necessary to make extended journeys inland by camel or donkey-back. The research of one's eyes and nose is enough without reference to yards of books in the libraries. You may see wretched, scabrous men, women and children with running sores on those portions of their bodies not covered by the filthy rags they call clothes, victims of syphilis, leprosy, tuberculosis and a multitude of intestinal diseases. They are undernourished, underpaid, ill-housed and illiterate.

Iraq affords a good example of the kind of government Arab leaders provide for their people. Iraq is a

ALLAH   141

large country with a population of only 3,500,000 people. At least 90 per cent of them live on a sub-human standard. Of these, three-quarters suffer from chronic malnutrition and the rest cannot even be called under-nourished. They are living dead.

Of the remaining 10 per cent of the population of Iraq, about 2 per cent are fabulously wealthy and 8 per cent comprise the bourgeois class of shopkeepers who manage to eke out a precarious but belly-filling existence. The reason for the plight of the Iraqi people may be found in the corruption of their ruling class. Ever since the last war British, Dutch and American oil companies have poured into the coffers of the government about $100,000,000 in royalties on oil concessions and in various forms of grants for road construction, education and health programs. This was cream for the pashas. The paupers never saw any of it.

Despite the anti-social attitude of Arab leadership, and notwithstanding the Arabs' open antagonism to democracy's cause in the recent war, Anglo-American policy is clearly aimed at supporting Pan-Arabism as though there existed, in truth, an Arab federation or an Arab civilization whose precepts of government parallel our own.

Yes, there is a so-called Arab League with representatives in Washington, London and other capitals who loudly make demands, voice imprecations and draft protests. But the voices heard by President Truman and Premier Attlee are not the voices of the Arab people, merely those of Arab potentates who speak for the upper 2 per cent and not for the masses.

America and Britain, in their almost fawning courtship of the Arabs, behave as though the Arabs were a compact, united mass. Perhaps they are, for the moment. But what holds them together is the cement of xenophobia directed, for the moment, against the Jews. Tomorrow it might be against the British or the Americans as, quite recently, it was directed against the French in Lebanon. A man who really knew the Arabs and who was their sincere friend, Colonel T. E. Lawrence, on this point frankly admitted in his writing that when people talk of Arab unity in "confederation or empires" they talk "fantastically." The Arabs' tribal and dynastic antagonisms are known to be such as to cause one to look elsewhere than in the power of Arab unity for the reason for Anglo-American appeasement of the Arabs.

The postwar history of World War I provides the answer. King Hussein of the Hedjaz, like Ibn Saud and to a lesser extent Farouk today, then had delusions of grandeur about an Arab empire. He was encouraged by the British, despite their own Lawrence's negative estimate of the possibilities of an Arab union. Then, as now, the British wanted to be sure of their domination of the Middle East, the frontier with Russia, the land bridge between Europe and the Orient, the source of the oh-so-precious-oil.

There are other considerations—strategic and political and perhaps some which go deeper, such as a congenital inability on the part of certain leaders in London and Washington to distinguish friends from enemies—but oil is one of the paramount ones.

CHAPTER VIII: OIL

Oil is the most powerful single weapon in the hands of the Arab princes. With it they oppose the creation of a Jewish commonwealth in Palestine and through it obtain the support of the British as well as certain powerful financial elements in America. Potentates like Ibn Saud and his confrères in Iraq and Iran own two-thirds of the world's known supply of petroleum and possibly more.

The royalties from the concessions they have granted to British and American companies keep them in power. It is unreasonable to expect them to relinquish their property rights without a fight. It is utterly reasonable, however, to believe that it is a relatively simple matter for them to enlist the aid of the British in defending their sources of wealth and power.

British support of the Arab's cause is aimed as much against American exploitation of the oil reserve of the Middle East as it is intended to preserve for British oil companies the property rights already in their possession. Our presence as an oil power in the Middle East is definitely annoying to the British.

The aim of British propaganda has been to undermine growing American influence there, as any reporter who was in the Middle East during the war years is fully aware. British agents spread the tale, during the early negotiations for the construction of an oil pipe-line from Saudi Arabia to Haifa and Alexandria, that President Franklin D. Roosevelt was surrounded by people who favored the establishment of a Jewish state in Palestine and that if such a state were established America would be to blame!

On March 11, 1944, the London *Economist*, an important vehicle of British opinion, saw the pipe-line as an example of an American excursion into Middle Eastern affairs which showed "little sign of forethought and even less of any desire to coordinate American policy with that of Great Britain." It saw American policy as one of "dangerous unilateralism."

To understand, however, the magnitude of the weapon held by the Arabs and how it is being used against Jewry, and to understand oil's relation to the Palestine question, one must go into facts and figures and some of the history of petroleum in the Near Orient. Throughout the war an Anglo-American policy of appeasement of the Arabs was understandable if inexcusable. Today the war is over. There is no longer any virtue in appeasement. Today political immorality becomes outright criminality. In wartime one might argue with some sense that peace in the Middle East was essential to a steady flow of critically needed oil out of the Arab lands. Today what can appeasement mean but defense of the profits and income of a few hundred thousand stockholders as against the welfare and very lives of nearly two million Jews?

When he threatened to cut off oil supplies to American companies, Ibn Saud gave his hand away. He proved that the true weapon with which he hoped to frustrate plans for a Jewish commonwealth was not the claim to prior ownership of Palestine as disclosed in his famous letter to President Roosevelt, but—oil. The truth of this was borne out by a satirical statement in a Turkish newspaper last October—when the Arabs were rioting gleefully in Cairo and murdering Jewish children in Tripolitania—that "His Excellency, Mr. Gasoline, is in the process of vanquishing Zionism." King Ibn Saud was reported prepared to terminate all contracts with American oil companies—possibly with the help of several million dollars' worth of lend-lease goods and weapons supplied him by the United States—if America persisted in a pro-Zionist policy. One is moved to wonder whether this was due as much to Ibn Saud's own personal principles as to the fact that he had obtained, or had been promised, a better deal somewhere else.

Ibn Saud alone controls about a quarter of all the oil of the Middle East region. The ultimate potential reserves in the Persian Gulf area are estimated at a total of about 50 to 100 billion barrels as compared to the potential reserves in the United States of only 35 billion barrels. The oil fields of the Persian Gulf drainage area include deposits in Iran, Iraq and Qatar, Kuwait, Saudi Arabia and Bahrein. The estimates greatly exceed the proved reserves and there is much exploration work still to be done in the Persian Gulf area, but it is clear that in this relatively small region of the world, inhabited by backward peoples and controlled by highly personalized feudal governments, is concentrated at least two-thirds and possibly three-fourths of the world's "free oil."

The distribution of this oil is estimated to be roughly as follows:

Saudi Arabia and Bahrein......about 40 per cent
Iraq and Qatar ....about 30 per cent
Iran ....about 20 per cent
Kuwait .... 5 to 10 per cent

Through the Anglo-Iranian Oil Company, Great Britain owns the southern Iran area 100 per cent. Of the Iraq area the British own 56 per cent, due to the fact that Anglo-Iranian owns the majority share of the Iraq Petroleum Company. The British also own 50 per cent of the Kuwait region.

American interests, namely the Standard Oil Company of New Jersey and Socony Vacuum as shareholders of the Iraq Petroleum Company, own $23\frac{1}{2}$ per cent of the Iraq region. Through Gulf Oil Corporation, Americans own 50 per cent of the Kuwait product.

The Saudi Arabian area is owned one hundred per cent by American companies through the California-Arabian Oil Company, which in turn is owned by Standard of California and the Texas Company. The concession to the Saudi Arabian fields was obtained in 1933 and has until 1999 to run.

There are three important refineries in the Middle East, the largest being that at Abadan, owned by Anglo-Iranian and capable of producing 350,000 barrels a day. The second largest is at Haifa, with a capacity of 80,000 barrels a day, and the third is at Bahrein with a capacity of 58,000 barrels.

The California-Arabian Oil Company together with Gulf has been trying since 1942—or shortly after America's entry into the war and the need became acute for oiling tankers, war-ships and planes in the Mediterranean—to construct a pipe-line from the Saudi Arabian fields across some thirteen hundred miles of desert to Haifa or Alexandria. It was also planned to build a refinery at Haifa to handle 350,000 barrels a day. Standard of California planned to construct a large refinery at Ras-Tanura in Saudi Arabia.

The proposal to build the pipe-line for the intensive exploitation of the Saudi Arabian fields and, among other things, to conserve America's own resources, was submitted to the Army and Navy Petroleum Board. This body was responsible for making recommendations to the Joint Chiefs of Staff on petroleum needs for the war effort. The proposal was drafted with considerable stress on the need for effective government participation not merely in the construction of the pipe-line but in controlling the policies to be pursued in exploiting the oil resources.

The scheme was rejected by the Army and Navy Petroleum Board and a year later, in the latter part of 1943, another proposal was made for a government-subsidized pipe-line but without provision for government participation in or control over the operating companies. The board recommended the proposal to the Joint Chiefs of Staff and it was approved by them.

It is interesting to note here that the executive officer of the Army-Navy Petroleum Board was Commodore Andrew Carter, an official of the Shell Oil Company. Associated with him was one General Pyron, for years the president of the Gulf Oil Company. Presumably neither would go along with the idea of public ownership and control of an important oil pipe-line across the Arabian and Sinai deserts.

One of those backing the pipe-line proposal was Harold L. Ickes, the Petroleum Administrator for War and president of the Petroleum Reserves Corporation.

P.R.C. was founded in July, 1943, as an agency of the Federal government with a board composed of the Secretaries of State, War, Navy and Interior as well as the Foreign Economic Administrator. Mr. Ickes was appointed president of the corporation with the principal function of exploring and encouraging the national interests of United States in the petroleum fields of the world and to propose safeguards for those interests. The Reconstruction Finance Corporation was authorized to lend the P.R.C. up to $30,000,000 in the pursuit of that broad policy.

On behalf of the P.R.C. Mr. Ickes entered into negotiations with the Arabian-American Oil Company and with the Gulf Exploration Company concerning the construction of a pipe-line from Saudi Arabia by the United States government at a cost to American taxpayers of about $150,000,000.

Had this pipe-line been constructed under government sponsorship and ownership, a long step forward would have been taken toward the internationalization and control of oil supplies and the elimination of sources of friction and possibly even of wars. But it was not to be. The private oil companies vigorously and in the end successfully resisted the efforts of P.R.C. to obtain government participation in the development of the Saudi Arabian oil resources.

The existence of a pipe-line from Saudi Arabia to a

safe port like Haifa might have shortened the war in the Mediterranean and would certainly have saved millions of cubic yards of cargo space wasted in the long haul from the Persian Gulf to the Mediterranean via the Red Sea. But the advantages of a government-owned pipe-line are too numerous and too obvious to enumerate here.

Finally on January 24, 1944, an agreement was reached which provided for government construction, ownership and maintenance of a pipe-line system from a point near the presently discovered oil fields of Saudi Arabia and Kuwait to an unspecified port in the Levant. This was a masterful document! In it the government, despite the tremendous investment of public funds, acquired no interest in the oil companies themselves nor any right of control over the companies' policies except as provided for in Article 8 of the proposed agreement.

Just for the record we must interrupt here to state that the agreement was signed by Mr. Ickes for the P.R.C. and by F. A. Davies as president of Arabian-American Oil Company; J. F. Drake, president of the Gulf Exploration Company; H. D. Collier, president of the Standard Oil Company of California; and W. S. S. Rodgers, president of the Texas Company.

Article 8 of the agreement entitled the United States government to be informed of all negotiations by the companies with any foreign government. The United States government also retained a veto power on sales by the companies to foreign nationals or governments if such sales were deemed against the interests of the United States. In addition Clause 8 provided that:

"The commercial and other policies and practices of

the companies would conform to the foreign policy of the United States."

Clause 2 of the proposed agreement contained some interesting stipulations. It said:

In the execution and performance of this agreement, it is the desire and intention of the parties not only to promote and assist in the development of petroleum in the areas affected by this agreement, but also to promote the interests of the governments of such areas, and to respect their sovereignty and protect their rights. It is the desire of the United States that American nationals that enjoy privileges with respect to petroleum in countries under foreign governments shall have an active concern for the peace and prosperity of such countries and shall exercise their rights with due regard to the rights, including that of political integrity, of the governments of such countries.

The clause imposes active and positive duties upon the oil companies involved, and it is not stretching the imagination to visualize Honest Harold Ickes pounding the conference table to see to its inclusion in the agreement. The clause is, however, susceptible of various interpretations. The possibility arises of local political intervention in the areas through which the pipe-line would pass. Whose rights are to be protected? What would be the nature of the sovereignty to be respected?

Specifically what would be meant by promoting "the interests of the government of" Palestine? Would the companies insist on maintaining the status quo, including the policy of the White Paper closing Palestine to Jewish immigration? The implications of the language contained in Clauses 2 and 8 of the agreement for the construction of a pipe-line across the Arabian desert through Transjordania and Palestine to the sea are many and far-reaching, economic as well as political.

Article 8 could be interpreted to mean, for example, that wage payments, working conditions and operational policy generally would need to conform to whatever policy is laid down by the United States government. It could open the way, in view of America's legal commitments to support a Jewish commonwealth in Palestine, for Jewish claims for the sale of oil in the Holy Land at reasonable prices and a general upward revision of wage scales and living standards.

With public announcement of the pipe-line scheme, proponents laid stress on the alleged rapid exhaustion of oil reserves in the western hemisphere. The suggestion was made that our oil reserves would meet consumption needs only for another fifteen years. This country could not, it was argued, "oil another war." Its position in the world of tomorrow depended on the development of foreign oil resources. Opposition developed quickly and came from two quarters:

On the one hand some fifty-five oil companies which stood to derive no benefit from the pipe-line and whose interests are concentrated in this hemisphere, objected strenuously to the construction of any pipe-line with the help of public funds. These companies are interested in selling their own product at the highest price. They are concerned about the effect on their interests—primarily in the western hemisphere fields.

Public opposition by these companies was, however, based on different grounds. A memorandum setting these out in detail was prepared for the National Oil Policy Committee of the Petroleum Industry War Council, by Mr. George A. Hill, Jr., of Houston, Texas. It contained arguments subsequently reflected in a good deal of controversy in the press. Exception was taken to the suggestion that sources of supply in the United States are likely to be exhausted within the reasonably near future. Wallace Pratt, director of Standard Oil of New Jersey, asserted that our reserves will last another hundred years. Others offered much higher estimates. It was argued that insufficient account was taken of continuing discoveries of new deposits; that the same scare was raised at the end of the last war and proved likewise unjustified.

In any case, the opponents said, "the pipe-line would be unnecessary. There would be ample tanker tonnage available at the end of the war." Also the proposed government construction was in conflict with American ideas of free enterprise and that neither on grounds of security nor of public policy could the proposal be justified. Emphasis was placed on the argument that the pipe-line involved a foreign commitment outside the western hemisphere in the midst of war, for strictly postwar purposes, and that it marked the beginning of an interventionist American foreign policy.

It is a foreign commitment by the United States [the memorandum stated], involving the physical occupation and utilization of a part of the territory of certain kingdoms, sultanates, sheikdoms, mandates, protectorates, neutral territories and areas involved in boundary disputes, over 1000 miles in distance ... and in which area there is embodied all of the political ailments incident to Arab nationalism, Pan-Arabism, Pan-Islamism, Koranic law, the Jewish-Arab feud, Zionism, remnant of Turkish influence in the old Ottoman Empire, Russo-Turkish-British relationship and rivalries, British foreign policy with respect to the Suez Canal and the Gulf of Aden and the Persian Gulf....

A second group which opposed the present pipe-line agreement did so on entirely different grounds. They included many representatives of liberal public opinion in this country. Expression was given to their point of view in an important speech by Representative Jerry Voorhis of California, in the House, on February 21, 1944. This group accepted the need for building up America's oil reserves by development of oil reserves abroad, but feared the growth of an irresponsible oil imperialism if the present proposal for exploitation by private companies should go through. The members of this group accordingly objected to the P.R.C. agreement as written, on the ground that it is essential that an enterprise of this kind, with all its international ramifications, should ultimately be controlled by the United States government. They favored construction of the pipe-line but subject to effective governmental participation in the exploitation of the concessions.

The 66-year concession granted by Ibn Saud to American rather than to British or any other foreign companies was the result of Ibn Saud's feeling that he had no reason to fear American economic and political penetration of his country. A considerable portion of Saudi Arabia's revenue is attributable to the sums paid for these concessions. Most of the balance comes from a subsidy from the British (a million pounds yearly) and from the revenues derived from the annual Mecca pilgrimage. The last-named source of income was greatly reduced as a result of wartime transportation difficulties. This undoubtedly added considerably to the financial difficulties of the Saudi Arabian monarch. The United States and British governments agreed to help finance Ibn Saud. Since Saudi Arabia was under the influence of the British, the financing arrangement was carried out through an advance by the United States government to the British with the understanding that $25,000,000 would go to the king. A somewhat different version of this story is that the amount was paid Ibn Saud by the United States government to counter subsidies paid him by the British government and to assist American oil companies in keeping their monopoly. Whether or not this money was paid will probably become a subject of congressional inquiry.

The visit to Ibn Saud by an American military mission under Major-General Ralph Royce to study "economic, public health, military and communication problems" in Saudi Arabia was publicly announced in December, 1943, and subsequently, in March, 1944, General Royce again visited Saudi Arabia and delivered an initial "token" shipment of lend-lease munitions, as well as a payment of $1,250,000 in Saudi Arabian coins, minted in the United States. Prior to this, a delegation from Saudi Arabia, headed by the two sons of King Ibn Saud, visited this country and were entertained by the government and by the Standard Oil Company of California.

Clearly the construction of an American government-owned and -operated pipe-line in territories directly or indirectly controlled by the British has important political implications. A number of reports suggest irritation that the plan should be developed without consultation between the Allied governments; anxiety exists too over the strategic implications of the pipe-line, with emphasis on a possible American naval base in the Mediterranean.

Despite statements to the contrary, there was no doubt, as this book was being written, that Britain and America were engaged in an undercover struggle of some intensity in the Middle East. That Ibn Saud was seeking to establish close oil relations with Great Britain by the appointment of a British petroleum adviser, was a significant index of the nature of this struggle.

The bargaining cards, however, were largely in America's strong economic hands. Britain needed some $5,-000,000,000 with which to rehabilitate its industries, restore its productivity and regain its world markets. America would benefit from lending the funds to Britain. But it was clear last winter that the United States would lend the money only with certain definite provisos about free trade, the lowering of tariff barriers against American goods, and freedom of access to sources of raw materials.

When built, the pipe-line would furnish oil to the European and Near Eastern markets. According to Mr. Ickes its construction would take "all of two years." Its effect would be to free Caribbean oil for western hemisphere uses. What result this would have on the price structure of western hemisphere oil is uncertain but is a major factor in the objections of the independent companies to the whole scheme.

The question has arisen as to the status of the Jewish Agency's demand that it be consulted on a question so vitally affecting the future of the Jewish National Home as does the pipe-line proposal. In terms of Article 4 of the mandate, the Jewish Agency is "recognized as a public body for the purpose of advising and cooperating with the Administration of Palestine in such economic, social and other matters as may affect the establishment of the Jewish National Home and the interests of the Jewish population in Palestine, and, subject always to the control of the Administration, to assist and take part in the development of the country." Article 11 of the mandate provides further:

"The Administration may arrange with the Jewish Agency mentioned in Article 4 to construct or operate, upon fair and equitable terms, any public works, services and utilities, and to develop any of the natural resources of the country, insofar as these matters are not directly undertaken by the Administration."

Article 11 was clearly intended to give the Jewish Agency a preferential status and entitles the administration to arrange or not, as it sees fit, for the Agency's participation in the construction and operation of public works and utilities and in the development of any of the country's natural resources.

In the event that the pipe-line is built, the character of the economic arrangements made in connection therewith will be of the utmost importance for the development of Palestine and the Jewish National Home. The future of Jewish industry in Palestine is closely linked with the question of cheap power—above all, of cheap fuel. Experience with the Iraq pipe-line is very revealing. No provision was made in the Iraq petroleum agreement for sale of the oil at the Haifa outlet at a fair price, or indeed of any oil at all, with the result that the British-controlled oil cartel maintains the price of oil in Palestine at a figure that is altogether excessive.

Again, while in the convention with the Iraq Petroleum Company various special fees and privileges were granted the company (including freedom from all duties on transit of its petroleum and petroleum products, exemption from all duties on all imports which it requires, special railroad rates for its freight and complete exemption from "property tax, income tax, or any levy or fiscal charge of any sort"), no counterbalancing stipulations were made with regard to the use of local materials, the wages to be paid to local labor, or the sale in Palestine of petroleum products with some relation to cost. In Syria, by contrast, definite commitments were obtained from the I.P.C. for the provision of oil and by-products at special rates to the Arab population!

It may be seen from all this that America has vital interests in Palestine. It needs a peaceful Palestine as much as Britain does. The belief that the way to keep peace in the Holy Land is to appease the Arabs is nonsense. When riots and demonstrations broke out in the Middle East last fall, fighting Jews blew up a Palestine railway at a hundred points.

The Jews of Palestine are armed, determined and ready to sell their lives dearly. It is reasonable to expect, from new and conclusive frustrations of their hopes for the establishment of a National Home, only their hatred and—violence. Arabs might puncture holes in a pipe-line. Jews who have served as engineers and technicians in the British Armed Forces can blow up entire cracking plants. If appeasement must be the keynote of American policy, it might behoove us to "appease" the Jews for a change.

Such appeasement would have the virtue of providing help for those who fought on our side in the war instead of against us. It would be a unique turn in American policy with its long history of support for Darlans, Badoglios and Francos.

AUTHOR'S NOTE: As this book goes to press there are unofficial reports from the Middle East to the effect that it may not be necessary to build the projected pipe-line from the Saudi Arabian fields to the Mediterranean. It has been found that there are some five hundred to six hundred tankers available which could carry oil from the head of the Persian Gulf to wherever necessary much more cheaply than it would be possible to build and maintain the desert version of our Big Inch. An interesting sidelight is provided by reliable reports that one of the sponsors of the transdesert pipe-line was an important American steel firm, with large holdings in the oil companies involved, which intended to provide the steel pipe for the line. If it is found uneconomic and impracticable to build the pipe-line another reason for appeasing the Arabs will be fortuitously eliminated.

The pattern of British behavior with regard to Palestine may seem to be full of inconsistencies but it isn't. A people who fought for the principle of self-determination deny it to the Jews. A nation which risked its life to prevent the triumph of Nazi Germany chooses to deny sovereignty to the Nazis' first victims. The country which rose in anger at the use of force in Poland doesn't hesitate to use it to ensure the continuance of the status quo in the Holy Land.

But there is reason in this seeming madness, for beyond the conflict in Palestine there is an even greater clash in which humble Jews and lowly Arabs are insignificant. This is the struggle for power in the Mediterranean in which the principal antagonists are Great Britain and Soviet Russia.

In an oversimplification, it is the struggle between unbridled capitalism—as represented by imperialism—and communism, and involves, therefore, not only Britain and Russia but the whole world.

Great Britain is an imperial power. It derives its strength from the direct and indirect ownership of vast, rich colonies, in addition to political allegiance and economic cooperation with members of its commonwealth. Without its empire, the principal source of its food and of the raw materials for its mills, Britain would be a second-rate power. Britain sees in Soviet Russia, or believes it sees, a threat to its imperial structure.

The conflict is not new. Imperial Britain felt the challenge immediately the Red revolution occurred and tried by direct intervention to frustrate it. In the years since, Britain has become increasingly conscious of the impact of that revolution upon men's social and economic thinking in its own country, in Canada, New Zealand, Australia and to a lesser degree even in South Africa and India.

It has absorbed the shock with a curious kind of political hydraulics which tolerates socialism and even communism at home but not abroad! It's all right for an Englishman to be whatever he chooses, but the same liberty may not be extended to colonials and foreigners!

Whether Britain is right or wrong in believing that Soviet Russia has evil imperialist intentions in the Mediterranean is irrelevant to the argument. The conflict exists. It contains the genes of war.

Judging by its behavior, Britain is convinced that Red Russia constitutes an economic and political threat. Its action in the entire Mediterranean basin—in suppressing the leftist republican movement in Greece and attempting to crush similar trends in Italy and elsewhere —is proof of the fears gnawing at Britain's imperial vitals and at the viscera of less-enlightened capitalists everywhere.

Out of these fears is born Britain's determination not to yield one square mile of territory in the Levant, the physical frontier between British imperial interests and the self-interests of Soviet Russia. As a vital segment of the Middle East, Palestine becomes in British eyes an all-important area of resistance to any alteration in the status quo. Palestine might be the first break in a general disintegration of the colonial system.

British policy in Palestine is merely a corollary of its policy in the Mediterranean.

The main highways of communications between Britain and its empire—between the United Kingdom and the food that goes into British stomachs and the iron and cotton that go into British factories—is the Mediterranean. On this waterway ships ply between United Kingdom ports and empire markets, carrying in one direction the raw stuff of industry and life and in the other the finished products of commerce and profits.

Britain needs the Mediterranean as a deep-sea diver needs the hose which connects him to the air pumps above. It must be certain that the vast, land-locked sea dividing Europe from Africa remains open to British traffic, and it has good fiscal reasons for economic concern. The war dropped Britain to at least a bad second as a mercantile marine nation. Its 23,000,000 tons of shipping made it once the ruler of the waves. It is left now with only 17,000,000 tons as compared to America's 50,000,000. With the reduction in its fleet went a proportionate cut in income from shipping services, formerly Britain's chief source of wealth and power.

The war cost Britain $76,000,000,000 and reduced it to the status of the world's biggest debtor nation where once it was the largest creditor country. Unless it can keep its empire together, it feels, it cannot hope to return to economic eminence as a world power. To yield Palestine would be to yield, Britain feels, a price in prestige and power in the Levant out of all proportion to what it would gain by the creation there of a new independent state.

In this broad program of ensuring the survival of an imperial system, Islam's leaders are Britain's natural agents. For they too feel the pressures gestating within their societies. The Jews, a force of change and progress, are feared by Imperial Britain.

But while the Mediterranean is for Britain a short cut to its empire in Africa, the Middle East and the Orient, it is also a westward route for Russia to the markets and raw materials of Europe and the western hemisphere. This is why the Soviets, lacking adequate warm-water ports anywhere, seek freedom of entry and exit through the Mediterranean by way of the Dardanelles, the Middle Sea's eastern gate-valve. These straits are in Turkish hands, but British-controlled. So are the Gibraltar gateway and the man-made petcock known as the Suez Canal. British domination of the Mediterranean is complete.

Only once in modern times was this supremacy threatened—by Italy, a Mediterranean nation, and by Germany, which sought to become a Mediterranean power, with entry into the sea affording a short route to the Orient via the Adriatic. With the defeat of Italy and Germany the possibility of danger to Britain's life-line from those quarters was removed perhaps forever. Fascism's and Nazism's bids for imperial power were crushed.

Now the British are worried about the communist danger. When British troops intervened in the Greek civil war in the winter of 1944, Winston Churchill told Commons it was to prevent the rise there of a "communist dictatorship." For years the Nazis and the Fascists said that *they* were fighting communism. British preoccupation with the identical Red menace provides one of the more tragic fruits of the war.

When Europe's Axis powers said they were fighting communism on the continent and in the world they meant Soviet Russia. So, apparently, does Britain. The Axis did a good job of selling the idea abroad that they and their satellites constituted a dike against bolshevism, and the mounting evidence of both Britain's and America's antagonism toward Russia indicates a major posthumous victory for Adolf Hitler.

So far Russia, motivated by a desire to make certain it will not again be attacked from the west, has gained an advantage in the desperate diplomatic contest for power in those areas where capitalism and communism come into direct contact. Poland, Rumania, Hungary, Bulgaria and Yugoslavia have fallen into the Russian sphere of influence, partly because they lay in the USSR's assigned military area of operations, but chiefly because it was politically natural for Moscow to support the anti-Fascist leftwing movements in those countries. In Great Britain's and our own military theater in Western Europe and the Mediterranean, we failed to support our friends, the anti-Fascists, and dealt with our enemies.

Is Europe, however, actually going communist? The evidence is against it. To begin with, it is folly to believe that communist regimes in the old Marxist sense are possible—in Mediterranean Europe particularly. Syndicalism might work in Spain, modified socialism might eventuate in France and perhaps even in Italy, and some republican form with socialist modifications would suit the Greek temperament. Otherwise, there isn't a nation in that part of Europe washed by the Mediterranean, in North Africa or the Levant, where communism, with its submersion of individualism, could or would work.

During the Nazi occupation the resistance movements everywhere were organized and led largely by people known as communists. This does not mean, however, that these movements were communistic. All shades of political beliefs rallied around the communists, and the Marxists, especially in Greece, Italy and France, were obliged to submerge whatever purely communist objectives they might have had into the will of the majority, for the purpose of (1) direct action against the Axis enemy and (2) revolution against their homegrown Nazis and Fascists. Essentially, because it helped us to liberate Europe and to defeat the Axis, this was a democratic revolution.

The Mediterranean races particularly love personal freedom too well to submit to the regimentation and self-sacrifices which communism demands. The cry of communism raised in the Mediterranean frightens the propertied rich, the landowners, the big industrialists —the few who have so much—and enlists their support against the many who have so little. As a result, Fascism and Nazism, together representing the evils which this war was to extirpate, might find a way to survive. If this happens it will be the worst betrayal of the common people of the Mediterranean and Europe in their entire history.

The British—and some Americans—were somewhat surprised to find a revolutionary spirit among Europeans. In Italy and Greece it was proved that while our military logistics were excellent, our political logistics were something less than adequate. We just didn't seem to be able to supply the one thing the people most wanted: some of the democracy we fought for. We seem even less able to supply it in Palestine for a people who gave infinitely more to the Allied victory than most of Europe's resistance movements. In deed, at least, they gave more than all combined—5,000,000 lives.

It isn't remarkable that the Mediterranean is once more the setting for the drama of a people's struggle for independence. It has been the stage of such strife for several thousand years. Into its cobalt-blue waters empty the Nile and the Po, the Rhone and the Ebro, and with them the cultures and aspirations of the lands through which they flow. Out of its basin have come three religions: Judaism, Christianity and Mohammedanism, and at least two major political concepts: democracy and Fascism. Here the republican idea was born and here it fights now for survival.

Republicanism seeks to reassert itself in Greece and Italy. It is beginning to stir again in Spain. It is striving to emerge in Palestine. But will we help it to live and breathe or will we trample it in the mad rush to man the ramparts against a new and possibly imaginary enemy? How real is the Russian communist challenge to British imperial security? Some measurements are possible. There is superficial evidence of a Russian "threat."

Before he left the Middle East, for instance, a certain Soviet minister to Cairo visited the half-dozen institutions of the Russian Orthodox Church in Palestine.

Whiskered White Russian monks and tremulous nuns feasted him, saluted him and, through him, sent their benedictions to Father Stalin.

With the air of a man who knew what he was doing and why, the diplomat visited in turn the monasteries and convents at 'Ain Karim, Jerusalem, Hebron, Jericho, Mount Carmel and Safed. At Safed, he was introduced to an old nun whose watery eyes had seen the glory and affluence of her church under the czars, had known the dark days of the Revolution and lean years of Soviet atheism, when the flow of peasant kopecks ceased and the Church's properties rotted with disrepair. The nun was one hundred years old.

The man who stood before her was in his vigorous early middle age, short, well-dressed and spectacled. There was something faintly professorial about him, but he was at the same time warm, kindly and respectful. He had brought money to the institution and had taken charge of its and the others' welfare.

"When are you returning to Moscow?" the old nun asked, holding the Russian's hands in both her own.

"Tomorrow, little mother," he replied.

"And when you are gone, who will protect me?" worried the nun.

"Father Stalin and myself," he reassured her. "If you are in trouble, send me a telegram and I will return."

In the chancelleries, legations, salons and cafés of the Middle East, the story of the Red diplomat's visit with the aged nun was told with mixed emotions. Most diplomats, merchants and journalists related it as "alarming proof" of Russia's new imperialism, usually with a "don't say I didn't warn you" air.

Recent events in Iran provided the stokers of Anglo-Russian ill-will with fuel for their inflammatory propaganda. A revolutionary uprising occurred in the northwestern portion of the country adjoining the Russian Azerbaijan. The revolution was aimed at the overthrow of the Teheran government, whose corruption and undemocratic mechanics were described in an earlier chapter.

The revolutionists were members of the new Democratic party, or "Tudeh," an offshoot of the old Iranian Communist party. This in itself was not as significant as the fact that the rebellion took place in territory which, throughout the war, had been occupied by the U.S.S.R. It was through this area that American lend-lease supplies traveled into Russia over a tortuous G.I.-built railroad from Teheran via Tabriz and Dzhulfa along the escarpments and cliffs of the Elburz Mountains.

Immediately the revolt broke out, the Teheran government charged that the Soviets supplied the rebels with arms. Moscow's *Izvestia* as promptly denied the charges. You may take your choice as to which side you care to believe, remembering only that the uproar over the Iranian democrats' upsurge coincided, strangely, with British difficulties in Palestine. The revolt strengthened the hand of those who would hang onto the Holy Land as a bulwark against the westward thrust of Russian influence.

Undoubtedly the Russians did nothing to hinder the Azerbaijanis' revolution. Why should they? It is to Russia's interest to have a friendly government, which is to say a government not under the political and economic hegemony of Great Britain, in Teheran. Moreover the region contains—oil. The Russians have sought to obtain concessions to exploit the oil resources of northwestern Iran since they entered the area. The Teheran government, supported by British and to some extent American oil interests, objected but promised to discuss the matter after the war had ended. The war terminated, but still no oil talks. It could be assumed without too great a strain on one's intellectual capacities that the little revolution in Iran was merely an extension of Soviet diplomacy.

The trouble in Iran went back a long way to unsettled Anglo-Russian accounts dating before World War I when, as recently, the Russians occupied the northern zone (at least it was under strong Russian influence) whilst the southern part was a British sphere with a cushion area, a sort of economic and political no-man's-land, between them. Iran (then Persia) declared its neutrality in World War I, but it became a battlefield nevertheless. British ships in the Caspian Sea fought the Turks and drove them out of Baku, the oil port. Later the British met and defeated decisively a Bolshevik naval force.

In the tremulous peace of 1919 the British tried to foist a protectorate on Iran, but before they could do so the Russians beat them to it by negotiating, in 1921, a treaty of alliance with Teheran. Thereafter Iran enjoyed a strange kind of independence with Britain and Russia struggling for the upper hand. Britain, eventually, won out.

World War II followed a similar pattern. The country offered a corridor for bringing supplies from the head of the Persian Gulf into hard-pressed Russia. On August 25, 1941, Russia and Britain decided to occupy the country much as they had before. Russia was assigned the northern and northwestern zone and Britain the oil regions in the south and southwest. Both guaranteed to respect Iranian territorial integrity and political independence and were to clear out in March, 1946. America became a party to the deal, formally, in a treaty signed on January 29, 1942.

The conflict was over two Anglo-Russian objectives. One was political influence. Russia undoubtedly sought to extend its system of friendly governments just as Britain tried to extend its *cordon sanitaire* about the communist world and its peripheral allies. The other was oil. The Tudeh, the largest and most influential of Iran's parties, had favored exploitation of the country's northern oil regions by the Soviets. Iranians have had a sample of exploitation under the British. They're willing to try the Russian system, which promises socialization of the sources of natural wealth and presumably a more equitable distribution of the profits derived therefrom.

An American oil man of considerable experience in Iran, an executive of one of our biggest companies, is the authority for the statement that the Russians should have the oil concessions in the north. The quantity of oil involved is probably considerable—no one knows just how much there is. It is located in areas more accessible to the Soviet Union's markets than to those of either Great Britain or the United States. For the latter two nations to bring the oil out would necessitate the construction, at a prohibitive cost, of pipe-lines to the

Persian Gulf where it could be taken away on tankers. The flow of this oilshed is naturally toward Russia and not toward Anglo-America.

Should Iran, then, be a source of conflict between us and the Russians? Hasn't the Soviet Union earned a right to have equal access to the world's sources of raw materials? Should the oil wells of Iran be the wells of another war? In your reporter's humble opinion the answer to the first question is "no," to the second, "yes," and to the third a most emphatic "no." We should instead recognize Russia's new stature in this world.

The Russians, however, are as short-sighted as the British and ourselves in quarreling over oil. The scientists have given us a new source of power, atomic fission. It would be far more constructive for the Soviets as well as ourselves to pursue the paths to a new society which the Oppenheimers and the Fermis have opened up, rather than to jockey for political and economic and strategic advantages. Long before any of those advantages could do nations any good we shall be well into the Atomic Era, or we could be if men would stop thinking about atomic energy merely as the ingredient of a weapon. But this, of course, is a diversion. We must set aside the "what might be" for what very definitely "is."

Few are satisfied to accept the above and other bits of evidence of "spreading Russian influence" in the Levant and the Middle East merely as signs of Russia's resumption of its place in the spiritual, political and economic life of the world after an absence of twenty-seven years. Many influential Britons and Americans seem to prefer to regard Russia as an evil force determined to bolshevize the world. This mistrust is alarming if world peace and reconstruction depend on the intimate collaboration of Britain, America and Russia.

Russia itself is partly responsible for political differences among the three major Allies and mutual mistrust over postwar objectives in Europe. The Soviet Union's own diffidence about allowing British and American correspondents the facilities for free reporting has helped obscure the atmosphere of Anglo-American-Russian relations. To assume because of this, however, that the Soviets are gestating dark plots to bolshevize Europe, the eastern hemisphere or the whole world, is a dangerous deduction. It's dangerous because whether or not the world will be catapulted into another war depends on how well Britain, Russia and America get along in the next quarter of a century or so.

If democratic principles are abandoned anywhere in favor of communism, it is unlikely to be as much because Russia wills it as because social, economic and political forces already at work there will oblige it. And for the time being, these forces are not communistic.

Russia long ago abandoned the world revolutionary idea in favor of a more practical and more profitable *Realpolitik,* or a policy of cooperation with Great Britain and the United States, which would better enable it to acquire the stature of a great power. One of the things Russia had to do to achieve the dimensions of a first-rate power was to slough off the Comintern, Moscow's international machinery for world revolution. This, by the spring of 1943, it could afford to do—and did.

The Comintern was abolished at least as much because Russia desired the good will and confidence of Great Britain and the United States as because the Comintern no longer served any practical purpose. The revolutionary social, economic and political changes which were the principal objectives of the founders of the Soviet Union were already under way nearly everywhere. Russia moreover saw that the direction of those changes wasn't toward Marxian communism anyhow.

If Russia actually presents a "danger" it is not as a world bolshevizer. It does menace imperialism—more specifically British imperialism—but this relic of seventeenth, eighteenth and nineteenth century economic expansion is endangered as much by democracy as it is by communism.

Surely Russia cannot be blamed for the outcry against French, Dutch and British imperialism raised in Indo-China, the Netherlands Indies and Burma. The motive energy there was furnished by democracy and not by communism, by America's presence in the Orient, not Russia's.

Logic would insist, therefore, that Britain oppose the spread of democracy as vigorously as it opposes the real or imagined encroachments of communism. This is obviously an absurdity, ergo: Britain should last realize that imperialism and the democratic principles for which it fought so nobly only yesterday cannot be reconciled ever again in the new era which dawned with VJ-Day.

What really frightens Britain is the re-emergence of Russia from the darkness of the years between 1917 and 1942. In some ways it is the same old Russia. This is visible in the czarist cut of its officers' uniforms, the revival of decorations in the Russian army and in a thousand other small things up to the important business of its return to the religion of its fathers.

In the Middle East, perhaps better than elsewhere, it is possible to observe the refurbished Russia at work. Concerned for the present at least chiefly with matters of prestige and politics rather than economic penetration, Russia seems to be doing quite well. It has a fertile field in which to plow. The general European feeling that Russia won the war practically single-handed is rather common, for instance, among Egyptians. To Egypt's fellaheen, Josef Stalin is "Abu shanab"—meaning the mustachioed man. When a disgruntled laborer wants to frighten an employer, he says, "One day the Abu shanab will come, and I shall have my revenge." Pictures of Stalin are common in Arab shops where once you saw only the physiognomies of Mr. Churchill, General Montgomery or His Britannic Majesty.

Here Russian diplomats hobnob with royalty, kiss hands, click heels, eat from Limoges china and walk on rare rugs. They behave like arch Tories rather than rabid revolutionaries—like true representatives of a power which hopes to live and prosper in a capitalist world.

In Syria and Lebanon as in Egypt, the Russians have enjoyed social conquests. In Damascus and Beirut they were feasted and banqueted by the respective governments, and both formally asked the Soviet envoys to convey to Stalin their thanks for Russia's contribution to the defeat of Germany. With British prestige at low temperature in the hot lands of the Middle East, old-line empire civil servants raised their eyebrows and clucked their tongues, but there was little they could do.

While Russia enjoys wide prestige among the common people and some of the politicos-on-the-make in the Middle East, there is fear and trembling among the moneyed pashas. When news reached Cairo that the Russians had crossed the frontiers of Thrace into Greece before the British had landed, Bank of Athens shares dropped 10 per cent in the Cairo Bourse. The report was false but the shareholders rushed to unload, certain that Greek banks, with about $225,000,000 worth of credits held in London and New York banks, would be nationalized.

Russia sent a minister to Syria and Lebanon in the person of Daniel Solod, a personable fellow who was professor of Semitic languages at Leningrad University. Russia, unlike Britain or America, wisely sends diplomats into the Middle East who speak Arabic. One member of the Russian legation in Cairo, Abdel Rahman Sultanoff, not only speaks Arabic but is himself a Moslem. Sultanoff goes to the mosque every Friday and sees to it that he is seen. He is short and thin, with a long nose, and he knows the Koran by heart. From the sacred book he derives numerous parallels between communism and Islamic theology. To escape damnation, a good Mohammedan must share his wealth with his poorer fellow. Sultanoff's job is a cinch.

In Palestine, too, Russia finds friends easily. Zionism is probably the best example of applied socialism extant outside of Russia—and maybe even including Russia. There are other affinities. The Red armies liberated millions of Jews. In Jerusalem, the story is well known of how a delegation of Rumanian Jews handed to the Soviet general who had liberated them, a priceless Talmud to be sent to Stalin. Stalin diplomatically accepted the Talmud with a message saying that he would keep it together with his special copy of the Holy Scriptures, "for the Soviet has always regarded Jews and Christians as equal members of the human race."

There is no fear of Russia in Palestine. On the contrary. Palestine, disappointed with repressive British policy, will turn to Russia not only to secure a friend at court when the decision for a permanent settlement of the Palestine problem arrives, but possibly even as a vassal of the new Great Power now knocking on the eastern door of the Mediterranean. One prominent Jew put it this way in a talk we had one afternoon in Shepheard's Garden in Cairo: "We know how bad the British are and we will take a chance on the Russians if it comes to that. Anything is better than what we have." If Britain's intention is to "save" Palestine from Russia it might better liberate it and so acquire a friend rather than continue to intensify the enmity of a full third of the people of the country.

Little of the available testimony to Russian "penetration" in the Levant or of "imperial ambitions" in the Mediterranean is such as to provide a reasonable basis for British fears about the empire's safety. What evidence exists, as before indicated, is shallow and manifests Russia's desire to resume its one-time role in world affairs rather than any serious intention of upsetting other nation's applecarts.

What the Russians do in the Middle East they often do with infinitely more intelligence than their British or

American allies. Here is an illustration: Whereas all British and American legations in the Near East have commercial and military attachés, the Russians have none. They send only diplomats and professors. They impart to the Oriental mind the impression that they are interested only in the moral and political welfare of the people to whom they are accredited.

This has produced at least one interesting phenomenon. When Egyptian laborers have a complaint, they draft a memorandum to their employers and send a copy to the Egyptian Ministry for Social Affairs and one to the Russian Legation. The Soviets have become the unofficial champions of Egypt's workers. This, of course, is viewed "as through a glass darkly" by the British.

Russia's interest in Turkey centers about the Dardanelles and Istanbul, formerly Constantinople, capital of the Russian Orthodox Church. Its patriarch is first in the Orthodox hierarchy, with the patriarch of Alexandria second. Moscow's own patriarch is only fifth in the hierarchal line. Russia undoubtedly desires the reunion of the Greek and Russian Orthodox churches which split in 1589 following the quarrel between Rome and Constantinople. The Greek Church is powerful in the Balkans. Rejoined, the two branches of orthodoxy would form a powerful counterpoise to Rome's influence in Central and Western Europe. Russia's desires in this direction too are understandable in view of Rome's opposition to communism.

The Soviet's resumption of relations with the Orthodox Church is not merely an attempt to woo the good will of the religious nations of the world, but part of a bigger event in world history: Russia's restoration to the status of a Great Power.

As a Great Power which intends to pursue the inherently selfish but not necessarily belligerent interests the role demands, Russia must have warm-water ports, access to the manufactured goods and raw materials of the Americas by way of the Mediterranean and the Atlantic, the right to cultivate normal diplomatic relations with the rest of the world, and markets for its eventual surplus of manufactured goods. There is, however, little for the western capitalist nations to fear from Russian competition for some ten or fifteen years. In that time Russia will be busy filling its own people's demand for consumer goods and raising the economic level of its population. After that it is to be hoped that there will be enough world trade for all.

As a Great Power, too, Russia has every right to ask for and insist upon friendly border nations whose governments will cooperate with it for the maintenance of peace, rather than Fascist states which are at best "buffers" and at worst springboards for another attack from the west.

Russia's diplomatic struggle to ensure its own safety and prosperity in a hostile world has intensified the already aroused antagonism of British statesmen. This animosity expresses itself in many ways, and one of the more obvious is in Britain's insistence upon keeping things as they are in the Levant, where London sponsors independence when it is for somebody else's mandate and Arabs are involved, but opposes it when its own areas and Jews are concerned.

When it signed the Charter of the United Nations,

Britain signified its faith in the ability of the peoples of the world to create an international machinery of peace. Its diplomacy in the Middle East, particularly in respect to Palestine, belies that faith. It is the diplomacy of fear. It is the diplomacy of war.

For if Britain really believes in peace—or wants peace—it would show some magnanimity concerning Palestine. It is axiomatic that the stability of the world depends on continued friendly relations in all fields of Britain, America and Russia. If Britain desires a stable, cohesive world instead of a globe segmented into power areas held in precarious balance, it could help materially to achieve it by fulfilling its pledges to the Jews. This would prove that the signatures on the Atlantic Charter and on the United Nations Charter were genuine. It might cause understandable Russian suspicion of British motives to subside and in a resultant recession of mutual animosities, the Anglo-American-Russian cooperation prospected by the Moscow Agreement and the Yalta Conference could reasonably be realized.

Palestine is one of the keys to world peace.

As events moved toward their tragic dénouement in the Holy Land, the more wily Arab leaders strove, and successfully, to take advantage of British preoccupation with Russian designs in the Middle East. They conveyed to the British, through spokesmen like Iraq's Prime Minister Nouri Said, their readiness to sell out to the Russians in the event that the present overlords of Araby granted the Jews any further concessions in Palestine.

Predisposed to believe the worst and cognizant of the Arab's venality, the British chose to credit Said. At least they behaved as though they did. They dispatched some seven thousand additional well-trained parachutists and commandos to Palestine.

Could the Russians buy out the Arabs? Of course they could. The Arabs aren't interested in *who* pays them, merely in *how much*. It's entirely conceivable that they would switch their allegiance from the British to the Russians if the latter offered the proper monetary inducements. But such a switch would entail a Soviet commitment to crush Jewish aspirations for a commonwealth in Palestine. There is nothing in the Soviets' record to indicate that they would embark upon anti-Semitism as a part of their internal or external policy.

Would Russia try to buy out Ibn Saud and his noble colleagues in Araby? Assuming that it wished to do so, what would Russia gain? Precisely nothing. It would merely find itself with a war on its hands. It is inconceivable that Russia desires a war just as it is a violation of all logic to believe that either Britain or the United States would wish another world conflict in view of science's discovery of a means of exploding atomic energy.

To further reduce to absurdity the Arab political trick of playing Britain (and America) off against Russia, it is merely necessary to point out what would happen if, indeed, the Middle East came under Soviet hegemony. In such an order of things the pashas and the princes of Araby would lose the positions of wealth and power they now enjoy. Ergo: the Arabs don't want Russia in the Middle East and they are bluffing mightily when they indicate to the British Colonial Office, as Nouri Said has done, that they would ally themselves with Russia against Britain in the event of an open clash.

Let's give the Russians credit for some sense. They would want fighters for allies, and the Arabs—valiant and able horsemen though they are—cannot be considered a decisive military factor. When the British allowed the Arabs of Egypt to "man" the anti-aircraft defenses in Cairo and Alexandria as a sop to their pride, their participation was limited to doing the manual labor of passing ammunition and in aiming and operating not the guns but the searchlights!

The Arabs are not alone in seeking to make capital out of the basic antagonism between Britain and Soviet Russia. A small but highly vocal minority of Palestinian refugees in America, some of them distantly related politically to the Irgun Zevai Leumi and the N. M. O. terrorists, are also preaching the Red menace. Palestine, these say, must become a "buffer" state between Britain and Russia in the Levant. This is opportunism and flagrant jingoism, but it has made some headway among those politicians in Washington who might not be interested in giving Palestine to the Jews on moral or other grounds, however sound, but eagerly grasp the idea that an independent Palestine would constitute a cushion between Us and Them.

They, with their shortsighted counterparts in London, are the Little Men who may give us another Big War.

CONCLUSION

CONCLUSION

CHAPTER X: *JUSTICE*

What is to be done about Palestine is a question which doesn't individually concern Arab leaders, politicians of the British Colonial Office, exalted American Senators, special pleaders and pressure groups —but collectively all people who consider themselves to be civilized.

The problem exists because we, the non-Jews in every nation in every century since the Babylonians destroyed the Kingdom of Judea half a millennium before Christ, have committed against our brothers the Jews indescribable injustices. The Palestine problem of today is a heritage and a natural result of our own xenophobia, our own crass stupidity and bigotry and faithlessness.

The problem existed after the last war when, as now, there were Wandering Jews, unwanted, unloved. It exists now. The difference is in degree of acuteness. Today it presses more heavily than ever upon the collective conscience simply because there are more Wandering Jews than ever and they are more frankly unwanted and unloved, thanks to the Hitlers and the Mussolinis of the past quarter-century.

The Balfour Declaration promising the establishment of a Jewish National Home in Palestine after the last war was no mere outburst of the postwar idealism of the time but a frank, honest, considered effort to find a solution. True, it was merely a remedy—a patch on the boiler. It is no longer possible to patch the boiler. We must now get a new boiler. We must solve the Palestine problem resolutely, definitively and justly.

We must, at last, redeem the pledges of the Balfour Declaration. Somewhere we must begin to acquire the habit of keeping our promises. The cycle of faithlessness cannot endure forever. World unity cannot be built on the unsteady foundations of broken promises. It is no more possible to achieve a good world—that is to say a peaceful and prosperous world—if the pledged word is meaningless therein, than it is to build a happy marriage on ill-will and infidelity.

Arab objections to the fulfilment of the pledge of the Balfour Declaration come to mind. But are the hopes of Jews for a national identity as citizens in a Jewish commonwealth to be denied them because the Arabs "were there first"? Then the Indians have the right to demand title to Manhattan. Let us give Texas back to the Mexicans. Let us restore every area of the world to the aborigines who first owned it, and kill civilization altogether!

Is the Jewish dream of a homeland such as Jews enjoyed under the protection of the Persians in 646 B.C. to be extinguished on the altar of British imperialism or ignored in the scramble of the Great Powers for advantageous positions for another war? Then the Atlantic Charter was a lie and the Charter of the United Nations was a fraud.

Are Jews to be excluded from Palestine and left to the mercies of nations grown increasingly more inhospitable in the past twenty-five years of intensified anti-

Semitism whose immorality even Robert Ley admitted on the eve of his self-destruction? Then we shall not sleep.

"Ah," you might say, "but the transfer of some two million Jews from Europe to the Holy Land would be a Gargantuan job requiring many millions of dollars, millions of tons of shipping, and the energies of thousands of people to transport, house, clothe, feed and otherwise care for these people."

Of course it's an enormous job. The migration of large numbers of people is always a big job. But not as big a one as defeating Nazi Germany and Fascist Italy and imperial Japan. It wouldn't take quite as much shipping! It wouldn't consume anything approaching the $250,000,000 a day which the United States alone was willing to invest in the destructive business of smashing the Axis!

Here is a constructive piece of work for civilized peoples to undertake. Here is a task which in the doing would fill men's hearts with a sense of accomplishment. There are no data at hand for computing what the merciful labor would cost in money and time—but what if the price were, say, $2,000,000,000 or $10,000,000,000? What price Jewish lives? If the two million Jews were Catholics or Protestants would the cost matter?

Actually, for Americans and Britons who amassed their power and hurled it victoriously at the Axis, who learned how to move millions of soldiers like pieces in a gigantic chess game on the vast geographic board of the world, the business of transporting a few hundred thousand Jews from Europe to the Holy Land would be a simple one, once the will to do it were found. Most of the Jews in Europe are already "concentrated" in specific areas. They could be transported to Mediterranean ports in Southern Europe, loaded on ships and ferried to Holy Land ports. Camps could be prepared in Palestine and the Middle East. We learned a lot in this war about building barracks, emergency hospitals, even schools and recreation centers almost overnight. The same energy and imagination applied to transferring Jews to the Holy Land as was employed in fighting a war would make the physical task involved puny. Simple justice demands that the welfare of those trapped on an inhospitable continent be treated as a major emergency of our times.

That it is our responsibility to solve the problem dealt with herein—and by ours we mean America's and Britain's—is clear from a brief glimpse at the legal record which enmeshes us irretrievably in the destiny of the Jews. If moral and human considerations are invalid; if the contribution made by the Jews to a common victory over a common enemy as contrasted to the Arabs' complete indifference to democracy's fate may be ignored; if all other considerations can be set aside, one still cannot disregard the legal basis for Jewish claims to a commonwealth in the Holy Land.

From 1517 A.D. until the end of the First World War, Palestine formed a part of the Turks' Ottoman Empire. At the end of the war that empire was liquidated. This would have occurred one hundred years or more before if the West had united sooner to destroy it.

Religious traditions have moved three religious groups to cleave to Palestine as the place of their origins.

Of these, only two—Christianity and Judaism—can make proper claims to Jerusalem as their religious capital. The Moslem claim to Jerusalem on religious grounds is the weakest leg of their case. Jerusalem is properly the capital of Judaism. For the Moslems the capital is Mecca.

But to continue with the brief in defense of Jewish claims which links America and Britain to Jewish destiny:

In May, 1916, an agreement was signed between England and France known as the Sykes-Picot Agreement, after the negotiators—Sir Mark Sykes and M. Georges Picot. This provided that Palestine west of the Jordan and south of Haifa should be established as a separate entity under an international administration. This agreement was quickly superseded by the Balfour Declaration.

On November 2, 1917, Lord Balfour, then Secretary of State for Foreign Affairs in the British government, issued his now famous declaration. It is worth repeating:

His Majesty's Government view with favor the establishment in Palestine of a national home for the Jewish people and will use their best endeavors to facilitate the achievement of this object, it being clearly understood that nothing shall be done which may prejudice the civil and religious rights of existing non-Jewish communities in Palestine or the rights and political status enjoyed by the Jews in any other country.

It could be argued that it might have been better if the Balfour Declaration had never been made. This, however, would be like wishing one had never been born. The Balfour Declaration exists, and perhaps rather than being an evil thing it is a potential instrument of salvation for a great people. The declaration was no quick and easy palliative for an unbearable political headache and, as Leopold Stennett Amery told the House of Commons during the debate on the White Paper in May, 1939—a statement of policy drastically limiting Jewish immigration to Palestine—the Declaration was "not a sudden, happy thought, a piece of war propaganda, meant to win the support of American or Russian Jewry—still less was issued in ignorance of the facts of the case in Palestine." Mr. Amery was a member of the war cabinet which adopted the Balfour Declaration, and he made it clear that it intended the Jews "to be in Palestine as of right, and not on sufferance, and no other consideration was to be allowed to prevent their free entry and free settlement as long as that entry and that settlement did not inflict direct injury upon the existing community, Jew or Arab."

His fight against the adoption of the White Paper by the government of the Arch Appeaser of our time, the self-righteous Mr. Neville Chamberlain, was in vain. In the same May of that fateful year in which Mr. Chamberlain realized at last that peace in our time was impossible, the policy was adopted. In a moment we shall see what the White Paper did, but let us resume first the narrative of events that tied America inextricably into the legal aspects of application of the pledges contained in the Balfour Declaration.

There was considerable opposition in Britain to the policy laid down by Balfour. All sides were heard. Finally, on February 27, 1919, the Zionists had their day in court at the Versailles Conference. Britain was represented by Balfour and Lord Milner. America was represented by Secretary of State Robert M. Lansing. One of the witnesses for the Zionists was Dr. Chaim Weizmann. Lansing asked him what he meant by a "Jewish National Home."

"I believe," replied the eminent Zionist, "that Palestine should be as Jewish as America is American and England is English."

Both Balfour and Milner expressed understanding of what Weizmann meant and both appeared pleased. Lansing, too, apparently understood and sympathized and must have so reported to President Woodrow Wilson who, on March 3, 1919, publicly stated:

"I am persuaded that the Allied Nations, with the fullest concurrence of our own Government and people, are agreed that in Palestine shall be laid the foundations of a Jewish Commonwealth."

Soon after, Field Marshal (then General) Jan Christian Smuts of South Africa expressed his hope that in "generations to come a great Jewish State shall be rising again in Palestine."

David Lloyd George was quite emphatic on the subject of what was meant by a "National Home" for the Jews in Palestine. The Balfour Declaration did NOT mean, he thundered on one occasion, merely that the Jews were to be given opportunities for colonization and settlement in Palestine, but it meant to recognize "the special position of the Jewish people in a country whose name the Jews made immortal." He had difficulty coming to terms with old Georges Clemenceau over the boundaries of Palestine. With a sweep of his hands Lloyd George insisted that the frontier enclose "the old historical Palestine, that is from Dan to Beersheba."

Lloyd George explained that the words "National Home" were used instead of "state" merely because the majority of the population at the time was non-Jewish. After the Jews formed a majority, he said, it would become a Jewish commonwealth.

On September 21st, 1922, the 67th Congress of the United States in Public Resolution Number 73 decided:

Resolved by the Senate and House of Representatives of the United States of America in Congress assembled, that the United States of America favors the establishment in Palestine of a national home for the Jewish people, it being clearly understood that nothing shall be done which may prejudice the civil and religious rights of Christian and of other non-Jewish communities in Palestine, and that the holy places and religious buildings and sites in Palestine shall be adequately protected.

From 1917 through 1920 Palestine was occupied by a British army of occupation. The peace conference in Paris in 1918 had made the final status of the land the subject of Allied discussion. The United States participated in the negotiations for the evolution of the mandate system. As understood by the Allied delegation to Paris, the mandate idea was formulated in Article 22 of the League of Nations Covenant which stated:

"Certain communities formerly belonging to the Turkish Empire have reached a stage of development where their existence as independent nations can be provisionally recognized subject to the rendering of administrative advice and assistance by a Mandatory *until such time as they are able to stand alone*. The wishes of these communities must be a principal con-

sideration in the selection of the Mandatory." The covenant further provided that the mandatory power must
render to the League of Nations conference an annual
report regarding the territory in its charge. The degree
of authority, control or administration to be exercised
by the mandatory power was to be explicitly defined in
each case by the Council. The annual reports became,
eventually, perfunctory things to which no one in
Geneva paid any attention.

In 1920, although no peace treaty had yet been signed
with Turkey, a special commission was entrusted with
the drafting of the proposed mandate. The United
States participated in the discussions and agreed to a
tentative text of a mandate for Palestine. The mandate
that was finally adopted by the League and accepted by
Great Britain provided:

ARTICLE 2: The Mandatory *shall be responsible for plac-
ing the country under such political, administrative and economic conditions as will secure the establishment of the
Jewish national home as laid down in the preamble,* and the
development of self-governing institutions, and also for safe-
guarding the civil and religious rights of all the inhabitants
of Palestine irrespective of race and religion. . . .

ARTICLE 6: The Administration of Palestine, while insur-
ing that the rights and position of other sections of the
population are not prejudiced, *shall facilitate Jewish immigration under suitable conditions and shall encourage, in
cooperation with the Jewish Agency referred to in Article 4,
close settlement by Jews on the land.* . . .

ARTICLE 15: *No person shall be excluded from Palestine
on the sole ground of his religious belief.* . . .

ARTICLE 27: *The consent of the Council of the League of
Nations is required for any modification of the terms of this
Mandate.* . . .

Every one of these precepts was violated in fact or in principle by the White Paper of May, 1939, and by the British colonial administration. The White Paper* restricted the immigration of Jews to 75,000 for the ensuing five years and permitted the entry into Palestine of 25,000 refugees from Nazi-Fascist persecutions. All but approximately fifteen hundred of the entry permits were used by the winter of 1945.

Obviously the medicine was inadequate to the illness. Between 1939 and 1946 the number of refugees doubled, tripled and quadrupled. Even in peacetime there were more Jews who wanted to go to Palestine than there were permits. Only the difficulties of wartime transportation left fifteen hundred unfilled permits by VE-Day. When the British government offered to allow an additional fifteen hundred to enter the Holy Land, the Zionists rebelled. At that rate it would take more than five years merely to move some 100,000 to Palestine. The illness had reached a crisis by November, 1945. Only the revocation of the White Paper could have cured the patient.

In Germany alone, 100,000 stateless Jews awaited permits to go to Palestine. They had no desire to resume the "nationality of their country of origin." And what of the stateless Jews of Poland, Hungry, Rumania, Bulgaria and other Nazi-ravaged regions of Europe?

The White Paper was issued as a unilateral act without prior consultation of the United States, although America was deeply committed in Jewish affairs and the future of Palestine. On July 24, 1923, for example, a peace treaty was signed with Turkey and by those na-

* See summary of White Paper in Appendix, page 209.

tions—Great Britain, France, Italy and Japan—which had been at war with her. America, however, participated in the drafting of that treaty as an observer, and was represented by Richard Washburn Childs, Joseph C. Grew and Admiral Mark Bristol. Article 16 of the treaty stated:

Turkey hereby renounces all right and title whatsoever over or respecting the territories situated outside the frontiers laid down in the present treaty and the islands other than those over which her sovereignty is recognized by the said treaty, the future of these territories and islands being settled, or to be settled, by the parties concerned.

Although the United States, which was not at war with Turkey, did not ratify the League of Nations Covenant, a bilateral convention was signed between it and Great Britain on December 3, 1924, affecting Palestine. The convention was ratified by both countries in 1925 and stated:

Whereas by the Treaty of Peace concluded with the Allied Powers, Turkey renounces all her right and titles over Palestine, and whereas Article 22 of the Covenant of the League of Nations in the Treaty of Versailles provides that in the case of certain territories which as a consequence of the late war ceased to be under the sovereignty of the states which formerly governed them, mandates should be issued and that the terms of the mandates should be explicitly defined by the Council of the League, and whereas the Principal Allied Powers have agreed to entrust the Mandate for Palestine to His Britannic Majesty, and whereas the terms of said Mandate have been defined by the Council of the League of Nations as follows [here is set out the Palestine Mandate to Great Britain], and whereas the principal Allied Powers have also agreed that the Mandatory shall be responsible for putting into effect the declaration originally made on the

2nd of November, 1917, by the Government of Great Britain and adopted by the said Powers in favor of the establishment in Palestine of a national home for the Jewish people . . . and whereas the principal Allied Powers have selected His Britannic Majesty as the Mandatory for Palestine, and whereas His Britannic Majesty has accepted the Mandate in respect of Palestine and undertaken to exercise it on behalf of the League of Nations in conformity with the said provisions, [therefore] Article 1: Subject to the provisions of the present Convention the United States consents to the administration of Palestine by His Britannic Majesty pursuant to the Mandate recited above.

Later:

ARTICLE 7: Nothing contained in the present Convention shall be affected by any modification which may be made in the terms of the Mandate as recited above unless such modification shall have been assented to by the United States.

Although the commitments were undertaken during the Wilson administration, the ratification of the convention between Britain and the United States came during Harding's time.

The mandate and the convention were violated with the issuance of the White Paper of May, 1939. America was equally guilty with Great Britain, for despite fine speeches of protest on the floors of congress, the United States as a government did not resist or seek to ameliorate the evil effects of the policy—as great a monument to Chamberlainism as the Munich Pact.

The White Paper permitted only a few thousand Jewish immigrants to enter Palestine regardless of the needs of some 8,000,000 Jews uprooted by the tornado of hate wherein 5,700,000 finally perished.

This, then, was the immediate result of the White

Paper. The document itself came into being as a consequence of the Arab outbreaks of 1936-1939. Their revolt was inspired by German and Italian agents. While Arab depredations were primarily directed against the Jews, they were also anti-British in nature and formed an integral part of Axis policy in the preparation of the war against the democracies. Chamberlain, with his White Paper, was appeasing not only the Arabs but the Axis!

A royal commission was sent to Palestine in November, 1936, and it made known its findings in June, 1937. The commission recognized that the "primary purpose" of the mandate was the establishment of a Jewish National Home, but it expressed the opinion that the mandate was "unworkable."

The British government subsequently proposed to partition Palestine, creating Arab and Jewish states and a separate area reserved for British administration. The plan died a-borning. The Arabs opposed it. British public opinion was unenthusiastic about the idea that the mandate was "too difficult" an obligation to be administered. The Zionists and the Jewish Agency naturally refused to surrender the rights of the Jews under the mandate and demanded that its terms be enforced.

In 1937 and through 1938, commissions and committees haggled over partition plans and finally there was held on February 7, 1939, a Round-Table Conference in London at which it was found impossible to resolve the difficulties attending any partitioning of Palestine. Partition would have meant the creation of a Jewish state and this the Arabs vigorously opposed. In addition to Palestinian Arabs, the confrères included—for reasons best known to the British Colonial Office—Arab representatives of Egypt, Iraq, Saudi Arabia, the Yemen and Transjordania! The conference, a euphemism for Colonial Office window-dressing, broke up and within two months, on March 17, 1939, the British government produced the White Paper.

The document was accepted by the House of Commons only after the government of Mr. Neville Chamberlain insisted upon its acceptance as a vote-of-confidence at a critical moment in world history when its rejection might have weakened the government's position in world affairs. Significantly the policy contained in the White Paper was formally disapproved by the Permanent Mandates Commission and equally significantly, it was never submitted for approval to the Council of the League of Nations.

The White Paper (and subsequent restrictions on the sale of land by the Arabs to the Jews) was enforced. Throughout the war years the Jews, in the interests of unity in the war against tyranny, largely accepted what was in effect a policy creating a Jewish ghetto in an Arab state. But Jews were being driven out of Central and Southeastern Europe into the Balkans and toward the sea like sheep to a precipice. Inevitably there was tragedy. It might not be amiss to remind the reader of one or two incidents which occurred in 1940 and 1941 as a result of the White Paper.

To enter Palestine under the White Paper quota, immigrants were obliged to have certificates. These, in the chaotic conditions prevailing in Nazi-occupied or Hun-threatened Europe, were impossible to obtain. Driven southward and westward by the Germans'

Wehrmacht and pressed northward by the Black Shirt bullies, the Jews were squeezed like cattle into a dipping trench in the Balkans.

Some found their way to Rumanian ports on the Black Sea and into Greece. There they boarded leaky, unseaworthy, pestiferous tubs, many of them not only without certificates for Palestine but without even passports or birth certificates. They paid hundreds of dollars, most of them all they owned in money and property, for passage on these steamers. In November, 1940, two ships—the *Pacific* and the *Milos*—arrived at Haifa with 1,771 passengers, all Jews, all "illegal immigrants." Hitherto such persons were interned, released and their number deducted from the quota. Now a new procedure was instituted. The human cargo of the two ships was debarked and herded aboard the *S.S. Patria* and ordered deported to the hellhole known as the Island of St. Mauritius. Sir Harold MacMichael, then the British High Commissioner in Palestine, broadcast a warning that even after the war such immigrants would not be allowed to enter the country.

The *Patria* lay at her dock in Haifa harbor. There was a mysterious explosion. Some two hundred and fifty of the passengers were killed and the death toll might have been far greater had not British soldiers rescued great numbers from drowning. The authorities interned the survivors and it is interesting to record that of one hundred young men released by the British, eighty-two immediately volunteered for service in the British army.

Later the steamer *Atlantic* arrived at Haifa with a load of seventeen hundred refugees. The passengers were interned at the camp at Athlit and when police came to remove them for shipment to St. Mauritius some of the men resisted, others lay down nude on the ground in the manner of Gandhi's followers. There were beatings and there was brutality such as to cause the Jewish Agency in London to call for an impartial inquiry. Nothing came of it. The cargo of the *Atlantic* eventually arrived at St. Mauritius.

On March 19, 1941, 793 Jewish refugees arrived at Haifa on the *Darien*. Most of these were Rumanian and Bulgarian Jewish refugees. At least half were skilled workers and farmers, eager to contribute their sweat to defeat civilization's enemy, Hitler. They spent their time not fighting but in a concentration camp and at least five of them became insane.

Finally there was the tragedy of the *Struma*. Its passenger list numbered 769 and included a large proportion of men fit for work or army service. Of these at least a dozen were skilled doctors and ten were qualified engineers. Several had expired visas for Palestine and many were property owners and students registered in Palestine schools. There were some two hundred women and seventy children, all of whom could have been admitted legally. Three thousand certificates had been issued to the Jewish Agency for the next six months. The Palestine administration however denied even children under sixteen entering.

The argument advanced by the British at the time was the old one about "security." It was a splendid wartime argument. The denial of entry to the Jew would prevent the seepage of Nazi spies into democratic soil. What a travesty! No such exclusion was made of known Greek, Dutch, Belgian, Polish, Vichyite French, Yugoslav and other non-Jewish quislings. (On the steps of the Shepheard's Hotel in Cairo in the summer of 1941 the author ran headlong into a renowned Greek Fascist ex-munitions maker. He had had no trouble convincing the British of his fealty to democracy.)

The British assisted in the transfer of tens of thousands of Polish refugees from Russia into Iran and some 70,000 of them, not all by any means good democrats, were quartered for a long time in Palestine. Amongst them were definite anti-democratic elements who later were discovered aiding the terrorist minority in the Holy Land.

Similarly the British found no rules in their little books on colonial administration to prevent the entry into Palestine of followers of the mufti. Only the Jews whom Hitler tortured, despoiled, degraded and killed were suspect. Petty civil servants argued against admitting the *Struma* passengers on the ground they would enlarge the number of consumers, although most of them were able to work and at most only two hundred were elderly dependents!

On November 10, 1943, the then British Colonial Minister, Oliver Stanley, declared in parliament that the White Paper of May 17, 1939, remained the accepted policy of the British government. Is it to be wondered at then that terrorism began to flourish in Palestine? The terrorist groups grew from mere handfuls of youngsters overcome by despair, who lost hope in peaceful attainment of Jewish salvation, into the large forces described earlier in this book. Many Jews, appalled at what the future held for them, joined the terrorist ranks. But there has been a change.

Now something new has occurred. The Fighting Jew
has emerged. He is the Jew who does not wish to be a
terrorist but wants to fight for the principles in which
he believes. His ranks are swelled by those who have
seen service and are skilled in the use of weapons.
Quietly, efficiently, in the manner of desperate men
with definite objectives, he has formed an underground.
He has left the ranks of the terrorists to join those of
the Fighting Jew. He, like his counterparts in France,
Belgium, Holland, Italy, Yugoslavia, Poland, Greece,
the Philippines and Indonesia, wants freedom and faces
the British in the streets of Palestine's cities, in the hills
and deserts of his beloved land to fight as did his
brothers abroad.

What is happening now in Palestine and what will
happen is inevitable. Perhaps it is only so that great
achievements can come. The dénouement in Palestine
is the arithmetical result of the addition and subtraction
and multiplication of our own iniquities.

In the weeks before and after the twenty-eighth
anniversary of the Balfour Declaration, Palestine became charged with the explosive elements of battle.
Balfour Day came and with it, violence. Arabs as far
away as Cairo and Tripoli attacked Jews, killing men,
women and children and otherwise demonstrating their
antagonism to the existence in their midst of a civilized
and progressive people. It is curious that Arab violence
manifested itself largely outside Palestine and that these
otherwise indolent people rose as if at a signal.

Their first move was to declare a general strike
throughout the Near East to start on Balfour Day. This
time the Jews, demonstrating a cohesiveness and pur-

posefulness never before achieved, struck first. On the night of October 31st explosions were heard in Palestine all the way from Dan to Beersheba. The country's railroads were dynamited at one hundred and fifty points. British police launches used for patrolling the seas for shiploads of "illegal immigrants," were boarded and scuttled in Haifa harbor. The dawn of November 1st knew dead and wounded. Two of the dead were Jews. Censorship blacked out the Middle East thereafter but it was known that the British had massed 50,000 troops in Palestine and were ready to deny Palestine to the Jews as they were prepared a year before to deny Greece a republic.

As the two sides squared off for a decisive struggle the mild and pleasant High Commissioner, Field-Marshal Viscount Gort, resigned. He was ill. From London came word that if the Jews resorted to violence in defense of what they considered to be their legitimate rights in Palestine they could expect only violence in return. Thus it was that justice was to be done in the Holy Land where Christ was born and where the philosophy of Christianity saw the light of day.

To help solve this new crisis in the affairs of man, America had little to offer. Once more we had no positive constructive policy with which to face a vital issue— although in the platforms of both the Democratic and Republican parties in the last election there were beautiful words supporting the Jewish aspirations in Palestine. But the election was over. Roosevelt soon after died. The America of Harry Truman could offer only vacillation and a vast confusion of thought and purpose, unresolved by the President's cautious sympathy with the Jewish cause and by his almost casual remarks to the effect that he had no intention of sending 500,000 American soldiers to Palestine to maintain peace. Unfortunately Mr. Truman's statement only served to encourage the Arabs to pursue to bloody conclusion their policy of belligerency.

Mr. Truman's request of the British government to permit the immediate admission of at least 100,000 Jews to Palestine was at best a fine humanitarian handshake. The reduction by 100,000 of the number of Jews, who died this past winter in the loathsome concentration camps of Europe, was no more than a gesture toward mercy.

Only the free and unrestricted resumption of Jewish immigration into Palestine could solve the problem and this President Truman was apparently not prepared to support, nor could the British see their way to allowing it. In other crises we were similarly unprepared. The results were costly and bloody. Eventually not only Spaniards, Ethiopians, Chinese and, most recently, Greeks died; but Americans and Britons and Frenchmen too. We were guilty, then, of gross disregard of our responsibilities as a great democratic people. We are guilty again in Palestine. Same crime. Different scene. Same purpose.

What is the crime? From Mukden in 1931 until Palestine in 1945, and onward until the problem is settled, the crime is simply this: the absence of an alert public opinion, mobilized on a worldwide basis, that can offset the forces of aggressive imperialism—whether these assert themselves in the West or the East—and that can be translated into effective political action.

What is the purpose? We have learned from the history of the League of Nations that mandates do not a purpose make. At this place in world relationships we cannot yet be sure that, as far as mandates are concerned, we have learned any lesson from the last war. If you win, the mistake under a mandate can remain a mistake. If you lose, it is a crime against humanity. The difference *can* be small.

If you are a victorious ally you can explain away a mistake. If you are the loser it is a crime. In Palestine the people stand to lose. The moment came, in the fall and winter just past, to redeem ourselves. We might have made the beginnings of a solution to the Palestine problem and so have made a true contribution to world oneness—*i.e.*, world security. But we didn't. We named another commission to investigate political, economic and social conditions in Palestine as they "bear upon the problem of Jewish immigration"; to examine the position of Jews in European countries where they have been "the victims of Nazi and Fascist persecution"; to "hear the views of competent witnesses" and to "consult representative Arabs and Jews"; and finally, to "make recommendations to the British and American governments to meet immediate needs either by remedial action in Europe or by providing facilities for Jewish immigration to countries outside Europe." Strangely absent in the announced purposes of the commission was any charge upon the commission to consider the relationship of peace between Arabs and Jews in Palestine to peace between the people of the world.

American consent to the British "suggestion" advising the creation of a commission to inquire into the situation in Palestine was low-level politics. The naming of yet another body of inquiry was postponement of a solution. It was intended, no doubt, as sound political strategy. The pledges of the Democratic party's platform were, or so the President and/or his advisers thought, no doubt, amply fulfilled.

But they weren't. Anyone even remotely acquainted with the Palestine problem knows that there have been innumerable committees, commissions and investigators. Their reports have never been acted upon before and there's no reason to believe that any new compendium of hastily gathered information will be acted upon now.

It is too late for "committees" and for "investigations." The facts have been apparent for many years. If, indeed, the governments in London and Washington wanted facts, these were at hand. But they didn't want facts. They wanted another delay.

What Harry Truman wittingly or unwittingly did by acquiescing in the British proposal for another "committee" was to approve the British White Paper policy of exclusion of Jews from Palestine in 1939. He was either ill-advised or had not kept abreast of current events.

For whatever reason, Mr. Truman missed an opportunity to assert America's true destiny as a great democratic power. There is hope, of course, that he will mend his ways. There always is hope.

One is inclined to be charitable in President Truman's lack of perception in this particular instance. British Prime Minister Clement Attlee's position is far more vulnerable. It was, after all, his Labor party which (when out of power, it is true) at Southport in May, 1939, declared its position vis-à-vis Palestine in these terms:

This Conference ... declares that the White Paper by imposing minority status on the Jews, by departing from the principle of economic absorptive capacity governing Jewish immigration, by making Jewish entry dependent on Arab consent, and by restricting Jewish land settlement, violates the solemn pledges contained in the Balfour Declaration and the Mandate.

The policy of the White Paper represents a further surrender to aggression, places a premium on violence and terror, and is a setback to the progressive forces among both Arabs and Jews. It also imposes new and intolerable restrictions on Jewish immigration at a moment when racial persecution increasingly divides the other countries of the world into those where Jews are forbidden to enter and those in which they find it impossible to live.

This Conference reaffirms the traditional support given by the British Labor Movement to the re-establishment of a National Home for the Jewish People in Palestine. It recognizes that considerable benefits have accrued to the Arab masses as a result of Jewish immigration and settlement. This Conference is convinced that under the policy of the Balfour Declaration and the Mandate the possibility exists for continued and increasing peaceful cooperation between Jewish and Arab peoples in Palestine.

This Conference calls upon the Government to rescind the White Paper policy and to re-open the gates of Palestine for Jewish immigration in accordance with the country's absorptive capacity.

If the "absorptive capacity" of Palestine is what President Truman was worried about when he decided to tag along with Premier Attlee's policy, he should have consulted Lowdermilk, one of the ablest agronomists in the world and one of his own civil servants. Any commission he may send couldn't provide more adequate data on the possibilities for Palestine's expansion.

Since the British Labor Party came to power the conditions described in the noble resolution adopted at Southport have become intensified. There has been a war. There are more homeless and unwanted humans called Jews than ever. But all that Attlee, now come to the premiership, could offer was again the tactic of delay—appointment of another commission. Attlee—when all this happened on his November visit to discuss control of atomic energy with Mr. Truman—was so busy convincing the conservative coalition in the American congress that his Labor government wasn't, after all, really very Red, that he lost sight of the larger humanitarian issues which confronted him and his cabinet.

Up to the end of 1945 the British government had not yet learned that the destiny of England lay not in the continuance of a policy of appeasement, but rather in the support of democratic movements everywhere, whether in Palestine or in Greece, Southeastern Asia or Italy.

In any event it was too late for committees. The Jews in Palestine were ready to die for the sake of the Jewish Homeland. It was no longer a question of whether strife could be averted but merely of when it would happen.

There were in 1939 nearly 17,000,000 Jews in the whole world. Of these, 8,939,608 were in Europe. Within a few months after V-E Day the Allied War Crimes Commission had ascertained that 5,700,000 Jews had disappeared from their homes during the Nazi-Fascist darkness.

It is to be hoped that not all of the 5,700,000 are dead. There is no way of knowing whether they are or whether they aren't. The evidence points to the worst. In Poland, for instance, there were 3,500,000 Jews in 1939. About 3,200,000 are reported to have been exterminated.

In Nürnberg, in a cell in a prisoner of war camp where he awaited trial as a war criminal, Robert Ley, a former Nazi Labor Front boss, confessed that what he and his master and their allies had done had been a "mistake."

Ley was a swine, a blackmailer, a drunkard and swindler. Like most of the Nazi and Fascist bullies, he was also a coward. Yet just before he choked himself to death with a gag, he had enough courage and sufficient reason left to write what he chose to call a political testament attributing the downfall of Nazism to German anti-Semitism.

I am torturing myself [wrote this creature] to find the reason for our downfall and this is the result of my contemplations.

We have forsaken God and, therefore, we were forsaken by God. We put our human volition in the place of His godly grace. In anti-Semitism we violated a basic commandment of His creation.

Anti-Semitism distorted our outlook, and we made grave errors.

Perhaps the Jews who died in the Black Years of Europe's recent history did not, then, die in vain.

SUMMARY OF THE 1939
WHITE PAPER

The statement was divided, after a general introductory note, into three sections. After pointing out the ambiguous provisions in the mandate as regards the obligations of the mandatory to the Jews and non-Jews, and after admitting that, though partition seemed to have been the best solution, from a practical point of view the establishment of self-supporting, independent Arab and Jewish states within Palestine had been found impossible, the paper proceeded to its three main sections:

1. THE CONSTITUTION

The government emphatically stated *that it was not part of British policy that Palestine become a Jewish state.* Indeed such a view would have been contrary to the mandate and other promises given to the Arabs. The government implied that the British promise of establishing a Jewish National Home in Palestine had already been fulfilled.

Turning to the obligation of the mandatory "to secure the development of self-governing institutions in Palestine" the government stated that it was determined to introduce self-government into the country, though it could not foresee the exact constitutional form which the government in Palestine would ultimately assume.

"It should be a state in which the two peoples in Palestine, Arabs and Jews, share authority in government in such a way that the essential interests of each are secured."

The government envisaged an independent state, but before the Palestinians would be ready for independence there must be a transitory period during which the mandatory would remain in control, and the people of the country would slowly assume an increasing share in the government. *The government offered that within ten years Palestine should be an independent state with such treaty relations with Great Britain as would provide satisfactorily for the commercial and strategic requirements of both countries in the future.*

"The independent state should be one in which Arabs and Jews share in government in such a way as to insure that the essential interests of each community are safeguarded."

During the transitional period both Arabs and Jews would be invited to participate in the machinery of government, and the process would be carried on whether or not they both availed themselves of it.

As soon as peace and order had been sufficiently restored in the country (after the 1936-1939 riots), *Palestinians would gradually be placed in charge of all the departments of government;* but they would be assisted by British advisers and subject to the control of the High Commissioner. These Palestinian department heads would be appointed from both sections of the community "approximately in proportion to their respective populations," and they would all "sit on the

Executive Council, which advises the High Commissioner."

Eventually consideration would be given to the question of converting the Executive Council into a Council of Ministers, and the status of the department heads to that of ministers of state.

After five years a body representing Palestine and the mandatory power would review the transitional period and make recommendations regarding the constitution of the independent Palestine state. However, the following provisions would be prerequisite to any treaty or constitution: free and secure access to the Holy Places and protection of property and interests of the various religious bodies in the country. "The protection of the different communities in Palestine in accordance with the obligations of His Majesty's Government to both Arabs and Jews and for the special position in Palestine of the Jewish national home." Provision for such requirements as to meet the strategic situation as might be regarded necessary by the British government in light of then existing circumstances. If after the ten-year period conditions would not warrant the establishment of an independent state and if postponement were inevitable, the British government would consult the people of Palestine, the Council of the League, and the neighboring Arab states before deciding on postponement.

2. IMMIGRATION

Although the government admitted that the principle of economic absorptive capacity of Palestine had been the immigration policy of the government since 1922, it pointed to the fact that nowhere in the mandate was that principle to be found, nor was there any indication in the mandate that the "establishment of a Jewish national home in Palestine cannot be effective unless immigration is allowed to continue indefinitely." In view of the Arab fear of increased Jewish immigration, any further expansion of the Jewish National Home by immigration against the strongly expressed will of the Arab people of the country would be contrary, according to the government, to the whole spirit of Article 22 of the Covenant of the League as well as to the specific British obligations to the Arabs in the Palestine mandate. The government, therefore, came to the conclusion that any further Jewish immigration into Palestine should depend on Arab willingness to receive new immigration. But if immigration would stop immediately the whole economic structure of Palestine might collapse. The government, therefore, would allow further Jewish immigration during the next five years (to May, 1944) to bring the Jewish population to approximately one-third of the total population of the country. This, however, would depend on the economic absorptive capacity of the country, and would amount to 75,000 immigrants over the next five years. As a contribution towards the Jewish refugee problem in Europe, 25,000 refugees (out of the above 75,000) would be admitted to the country as soon as the High Commissioner was satisfied that adequate provision for their maintenance was provided. After the period of five years no further Jewish immigration will be permitted unless the Arabs of Palestine are prepared to acquiesce in it.

"His Majesty's Government are satisfied that, when

the immigration over five years which is now contemplated, has taken place, they will not be justified in facilitating, nor will they be under any obligation to facilitate, the further development of the Jewish national home by immigration regardless of the Arab population."

3. LAND

In order to safeguard the Arabs from becoming landless in certain areas where there was no surplus of cultivable land, the High Commissioner would be given power to prohibit and regulate transfers of land. These powers would date from the publication of the White Paper, and would be retained by the High Commissioner during the entire transitional period.

The British government set out methodically to implement the provisions of this White Paper as far as the Jews were concerned. Immigration was restricted to the limitations of the White Paper, and land sales to Jews within the Arab zone, comprising about 82 per cent of the entire country, were prohibited. The reconstruction plan which the Palestine administration is preparing for the postwar period definitely envisages a Palestine based on the White Paper. The provisions for constitutional development have not as yet been realized and the Palestine administration is not attempting to implement them; the explanation would obviously be the abnormal conditions created by the war.

(1)

Date Due